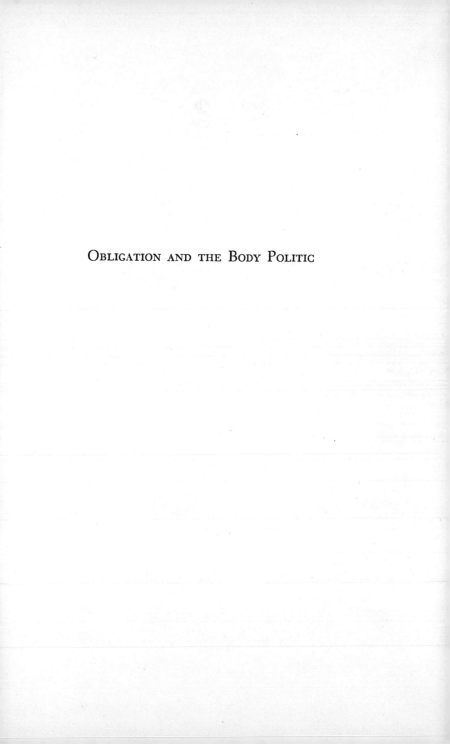

Obligation and the Body Politic

OBLIGATION

and

THE BODY POLITIC

by Joseph Tussman

New York   OXFORD UNIVERSITY PRESS

FOREWORD

This essay in political philosophy attempts to deal with problems and dilemmas as they present themselves to the member or the agent of a body politic confronted with the demands of his political role; it maintains the perspective not of the spectator, but of the actor.

The choice of this perspective reflects a commitment to an educational enterprise central to democratic life. A body politic which gives to each of its members a share in the governing process rests its fate upon the quality of participation. It commits itself not only to universal education but to education of a special character; not only to education for the private life but to education for the public role. And the theory which must serve as the foundation of that education is the theory of political obligation.

This essay is an effort in this direction. It is not exhaustive, and I am well aware of the tentative state in which it leaves many of the problems with which it deals. But it does, I think, provide a framework within which most of the significant problems of political philosophy find their place, and it does express and defend a point of view.

The fact that the approach is not historical and that there is only passing reference to great political theorists calls for a word of explanation. The issues raised here are not new. They have been posed and probed by many of our greatest minds, and it would be folly to ignore their work or dismiss their insight as outmoded. But it happens, in this day, that the study of political theory has become so identified with the study of its history that a 'political theorist' begins to resemble an 'historian of ideas.' This has not been altogether without profit. We now have interesting studies of the history and development of political doctrine and illuminating analyses of various political theorists. But at the same time the modern political theorist comes less and less to share in the enterprise of those he studies. *They*, for the most part, were analytic and constructive theorists; *we* become careful historians and scholars. There is quite a difference. And, eventually, learning what we can from history, we must make our own journeyman's effort.

This, at any rate, is an attempt at theory. It rests heavily and obviously on the creative work of other men. But, on the whole, I do not mention or talk about what I so freely use. There is, however, a case in which my dependence is so great that I must acknowledge it here. Since my undergraduate days I have been a pupil and disciple of Alexander Meiklejohn. I do not know how much he will find to agree with in this essay, but my debt to him continues.

J. T.

July 1960
Syracuse, New York

CONTENTS

1   *Political Behavior and Political Obligation*   3

2   *The Member*   23

3   *The Agent*   58

4   *Democracy*   101

    Appendix   NATURE AND POLITICS   123

OBLIGATION AND THE BODY POLITIC

1

Political Behavior and Political Obligation

THE POLITICAL RELATIONSHIP

Individuals and groups are related in many ways and it seems quite arbitrary to single out a particular relation as distinctively political. Fellow citizens are politically related; allies are politically related; and even hostile nations or states have political relations, poor though they may be. Let me say at once, then, that I am here concerned only with the narrower sense appropriate to relations within a body politic. The Soviet Union and the United States may be said to be politically related, but such relations do not constitute them a body politic. Even with the field thus narrowed there is no general agreement about what is meant by a 'body politic' or 'being a part of a body politic,' or, in this sense, 'being politically related.' I begin, then, with a brief consideration of some familiar concepts, one of which, I believe, will turn out to be more clearly adequate than the others.

The familiar characterization of government or of the sovereign as the 'supreme coercive power' calls attention to an aspect of the relation of the ruler to the ruled which seems to make government at best a necessary evil. By virtue of his power the ruler dominates the scene—coercing, applying sanctions, exacting obedience sometimes crudely through fear, sometimes more subtly through the use of temptation and the rhetorical arts. A body politic, on this view, is simply a group of individuals under the domination of a single power, obeying a common center of command, afraid of the same master. The political arts are the arts of control, of managing a human herd; the study of politics is the study of the struggle for power or influence, its seizure, organization, growth, dissipation, or circulation. To be a 'member' is, in these terms, to be 'under the control of'; to be a 'ruler' is simply to 'have power over'; 'leadership' is 'dominance.'

This is a familiar enough story and it is hardly necessary to make a case for the pervasiveness of power in human affairs. Its very pervasiveness, rather, raises a question about the propriety of identifying power as the distinctive feature of the merely 'political.' Apart from this, however, let me point out some of the consequences of defining a body politic as a group of individuals under a common domination.

First, there is in a body politic so defined no meaningful or necessary element of 'common good,' of common or public purpose or public interest. The interest of the ruler is one thing; the interest of the subject another. There may indeed be, sometimes, a common interest, but its presence is not essential to the existence of a body politic.

Second, none of the 'legitimacy' notions are significantly involved. The subject has no duty or obligation to obey. If he obeys it is out of inclination or prudence, hope or fear, or perhaps habit. But the weakness which subjugates him generates no moral claim upon him. Power, also, may allow the subject some scope, but this is a matter of indulgence rather than of rights. Nor does the ruler, simply by virtue of his power, have responsibilities or duties. He may use his strength kindly, by inclination or out of prudence, but strength by itself does not entail responsibility. Nor does it bestow legitimacy or 'authority.'

And finally, there is some difficulty on this view in making much sense out of 'political freedom' or of reconciling 'being a member of a body politic' and 'being free.' Law, regarded in this context as a command, is an assertion of power which the subject obeys perforce. Is freedom secreted only in the interstices of the law? Does 'freedom under law' mean freedom in what is beneath the notice of law? Does 'politically free' mean simply 'beyond the reach of law,' outside the range of domination which defines a body politic? I do not pause to deal with these questions here.

To identify the political relationship with power has at least these consequences: that one may be a member of a body politic without having rights or duties, that a ruler may have no responsibilities or duties, that membership need involve no sharing of a common purpose, and that 'political freedom' becomes a virtually self-contradictory notion.

Partly by way of criticism of the above view is the position that a body politic is a group of persons sharing a common set of habits or customs. To be a member is to share these habits, to be within the bounds of custom or culture. The denial of the centrality of force or power rests on the insight that fear is not, in fact, the cement that holds a group or a body politic together; that while it may be present its operation is sporadic; and that habit and custom embodied in institutions are the unifying and stabilizing bases of social life. Sometimes this view is expressed in the assertion that 'society' is prior to the 'state'—conceding the identification of the political with the coercive—but generally it leads to the treatment of political relations and institutions as simply a class of social institutions to be understood in the same terms, as a pattern of behavior.

A body politic is thus regarded as analogous to a language group. Being a member of a body politic is like being English-speaking; being politically related is like sharing a common linguistic habit. Rules or laws are less commands than generalizations, usage, or custom. Discipline is habituation; the sanction, disorder or outlandishness; membership itself chiefly an accident of birth and association.

Applying the same test used earlier with 'power' what do we find? First, there is some substance to, or perhaps shadow of, the notion of a common good. There is at least a common involvement in a complex process or enterprise based, presumably, upon a common need or a shared interest. And this may not be far from the politically interesting conception of the public good or public interest.

Second, the legitimacy notions tend here to be more shadowy than substantial. The subject has customary expectations, the ruler has customary functions. A student, on occasion, writes 'rite' instead of 'right' leaving one uncertain whether to criticize spelling or applaud insight. On this view it is not a serious error. Legitimate tends to mean customary; the obligatory is simply what is done; the 'moral' shrinks to 'mores.'

And, finally, as for political freedom—it is hard to know what to make of it in this context. We certainly did not choose to be English-speaking, but we would hardly say we were compelled to be. We are 'members' neither by choice nor by conquest, but by accident, growth, and habit-uation. Our habits are our powers; they are bonds only when we try to break them. And if law on this view is habit or custom what would 'freedom under law' mean?

The position roughly sketched here is, I think, an interesting and powerful one. Most Americans, if asked whether being an American citizen means simply being under the power of the government as a slave is under the power of a master would reject the suggestion. But they would not find too strange or hard to accept the suggestion that they are American citizens in the same general way that they are English-speaking. But useful as 'habit,' 'custom,' and 'institution' may be for the illumination of political life, they leave some crucial matters in the dark.

Saving the best for last, I come now to the notion of 'agreement' as expressing the core of political relatedness. A body politic, on this view, is a group of persons related by a system of agreements; to be a member of a body politic is to be a party to the system of agreements. The model is obviously the voluntary group or organization. A voluntary group is composed of a number of individuals who, in pursuit of a common purpose, agree to act in concert, putting themselves under a common discipline, authority, and obligation. The difficulty is not in understanding what a voluntary group is but in seeing the body politic as such, or essentially like such, a group.

There is a bristling host of questions confronting the claim that the voluntary group is an appropriate model for the body politic. Yes, it is the same old dusty idol, scarred and cracked by the lance of Hume, battered by the Historical School, mocked by every schoolboy who knows he didn't sign a contract. But we bow to it every time we demand the 'consent of the governed' and denounce the exercise of power beyond authority. It is still the revolution we cannot deny because it once was ours. Let me defer the defense of its relevance to consider here, as I have with the earlier notions, the relation of the voluntary group, or group based on agreement, to the conceptions of the common good, legitimacy and its kin, and political freedom.

There is no problem about the common good or public interest in the case of a voluntary group. It is organized for a purpose and *that* purpose is the public or common interest which its officers, on the one hand, are authorized to promote, and to which members, in becoming members, express their commitment, however limited.

Authority, obligation, duty, responsibility, rights—these notions not only fit into the analysis of a voluntary group but seem built into it so that it is hard to imagine an adequate account of a voluntary group which would not include a statement of the responsibilities and duties of its officials, the rights and obligations of its members, as well as the common purpose mentioned above. Since the basis of a voluntary group is agreement it should be observed that 'having a right' or 'being obligated' seems to relate itself more easily to agreement than to force or to habit. In other words, 'I have a duty to . . .' seems to follow from 'I have agreed to' in a way that it does not follow from 'I am forced to' or 'I am in the habit of.' This is sometimes expressed as the view that obligations are, or even must be, voluntarily assumed. To the extent that a body politic is regarded as a voluntary group there is, then, no doubt about the possibility, propriety, or even necessity, of making sense out of the general range of legitimacy notions.

The problem of political freedom, or of freedom under law, appears in an interesting light when the body politic is thought of as a voluntary group. Law is seen not as the command of the dominant power, nor as habit or custom, but rather as an agreement. To take a crude example: A 'No Smoking' sign in a public auditorium might be regarded as 'Don't smoke!' or 'Smoking is not customary here' or 'We have agreed not to smoke here.' If it seems strange to read an implicit 'we have agreed . . .' before a law, some of the strangeness wears off upon reflection. If I as a citizen of the United States have agreed to recognize the authority of the Constitution (assuming here the voluntary group view) have I not agreed to the delegation of some authority to Congress to pursue certain purposes in certain ways? And when, acting as thus agreed, it enacts a law is it so strange to preface it with the reminder that 'we have agreed . . .'? The essential point is that to the extent that law is a system of agreements to which I am a party, 'being under law' does not conflict with 'being free' unless, indeed, I consider myself not free when I do what I have agreed or consented to do.

In this tradition 'political freedom' does not turn on the absence of law but on whether the law is 'self-imposed.' And it is only in this tradition that one can make any sense at all out of 'freedom under law.' The demand for freedom under law is not the demand for an indulgent master. It is the demand that our social order be reconstructed as a voluntary group so that the law to which we are subject can, without irony, be treated as agreements to which we are all, directly or indirectly, parties.

Each of the notions considered above—power, habit or custom, and agreement—reminds us of an important feature of political life. Government, whatever else it needs, needs power. It applies sanctions, punishes, coerces, and enforces. But it is not to such power or to fear of punishment that one looks for the cement that holds a body politic together. Stability, continuity, and cohesiveness are largely the product of social habit and institution, not of commands and bayonets. But social habit, it must then be said, does not, by itself, account for the structure of authority which beyond the web of custom constitutes some of the most important and distinctive features of political life. For this the modern mind, at least, finds no real basis other than agreement or consent, taking the body politic as a voluntary organization.

Having briefly paraded these candidates for the leading role in the political drama, I suggest that we take 'agreement' as definitive and the voluntary group as the model for the body politic. I do so because, as was indicated above, this supports, as power and habit do not, a significant conception of the common good, authority, right, obligation, duty, and freedom under law. And this is decisive because education for political life—a crucial and indispensable enterprise—makes no sense without these notions.

Graham Wallas once characterized the great philosophers of Athens as 'training free citizens to exercise judgment on behalf of a conciously self-governed community.' This has always seemed to me an especially apt statement of what liberal education is—when it is what it should be. I shall resist the temptation to pursue the argument that the 'liberal' is the 'political.' The liberal college will continue to flounder from one morass into another until it rediscovers, in the task of educating the ruler, the central theme of its life. But whether this is so or not, the education of the citizen for the responsibilities of a variety of political roles is a pressing task. Political theory and philosophy are, at the very least, heavily involved in the problem of enlightening the activity which is itself the starting point of theoretical reflection and construction. I take it for granted, then, that a political theory which turns out not to be relevant to political education has failed us where it is most needed.

Put more specifically, political theory should have something to say to us as we set about the preparing of members of a body politic to meet the demands of the political roles they may be called upon to play. These roles are varied, but there is a basic division that should be made. First, to be a *member* is to have a status entailing rights and obligations which need careful analysis. The role of member is one for which everyone needs education. Second, there is the role of *agent*, of one who acts for, on behalf of, or in the name of a body politic. I use agent in its broadest sense without here distinguishing between the legislative, executive, judicial or other possible kinds of agents. 'Member' and 'agent' correspond roughly to 'subject' and 'ruler' or 'public official,' and so there is nothing very novel about the distinction. While, compared with the agent, the role of member seems passive, the member has duties and needs to act; I consider it an active role; but it is still significantly distinguishable from the role of an agent. One person can, of course, have a variety of roles.

Political education is education which prepares one to meet the demands of political roles. Political theory has, then, the task of delineating the general demands of the roles of membership and agency. This simply cannot be done without reference to such notions as rights, obligations, and duties, and without cognizance of a common or public good, however difficult these notions may be. And, because it alone appears to make sense out of these notions, the voluntary group—based on agreements—must, as a practical matter, be taken as a model for the understanding of a body politic.

POLITICAL BEHAVIOR AND POLITICAL OBLIGATION

I turn now to a distinction upon which this whole essay turns. There are two radically distinct points of view or perspectives from which political life or the political process can be studied. First, there is the perspective of the external observer concerned with the description of political behavior. This is continuous with the interest in prediction of such behavior since, of course, an adequate description may reveal patterns which form the basis of prediction. This perspective, intrinsic to most of what is called 'social science,' might, then, be called 'descriptive-predictive.' Brought to bear upon the political agent or decision-maker its basic question is 'what will he do?'.

But second, there is the point of view, not of the observer, but of the person (or persons) within a tribunal confronting his task. And this task is not *predicting* but *deciding*; the question is not what *will* I do but what *should* I do. I shall call this essentially 'normative' or 'practical' perspective, the 'perspective of action.'

These two perspectives, the observer's and the actor's, with their two kinds of questions, are not reducible to a single form. It may happen, not infrequently, that the answers to 'what will he do?' and 'what should I do?' will be the same. Actors sometimes do what they should do. But this happy circumstance should not obscure the basic distinction.

A single example may be useful. In a famous address to law students, *The Path of the Law*, Justice Holmes develops the theme that the study of law is the study of the behavior of judges. The lawyer must advise his client about whether or not he will be upheld in the assertion of some claim or demand; to do this he must be skilled in the prediction of judicial behavior. The lawyer's question is 'what will the judge do?' But this is only part of the story. The judge, manning the judicial tribunal, is confronted with a problem. He is not trying to predict his own behavior; he is concerned with behaving properly, with determining what he 'should' do. And that is quite another matter.

The difference between the perspective of the observer and the perspective of the actor is the basis of the distinction between a Theory of Political Behavior and a Theory of Political Obligation. They are responses to the distinct demands of prediction and performance.

I pause here in the development of the argument to touch briefly on several matters. *First*, the relation of these two perspectives to each other raises the traditional problem of freedom and determinism. The same activity, the activity of the decision-maker, is treated in two different sets of terms. On the one hand it is regarded as predictable; on the other hand it is seen as a kind of choosing. And the greater our success in predicting, the more inclined we are to dismiss the 'choice' as unreal or illusory. If behavior is predictable how can it also be free? If the judge's action can be predicted, in what sense can he be regarded as free to decide one way or the other? What is thus posed is the problem of 'free will.'

Resolving this difficulty to everyone's satisfaction is hardly possible, but something can be attempted very briefly. The conflict seems to be initially between predictability and freedom of choice. I say 'seems to be,' because the so-called problem exists at another level. There is really no difficulty in regarding an act as both free and predictable. If we know someone well enough to predict his choice we do not thereby deprive him of choice.

It is only when we try to explain *why* action is predictable that a conflict may appear. That is, if we try to account for predictability by seeing it as the result of the existence of some 'compelling' causal relation then we have on one account a 'choice' and on the other account 'compulsion.' And it is hard to see how the same act can be both free and compelled. The error consists in substituting 'compelled' for 'predictable,' so that an act which, unobjectionably, is both predictable and free seems instead an act which is both 'compelled' and 'free.' Since these are clearly incompatible we seem to have to give up either the belief in a causal order, upon which the observer depends, or the belief in the reality of the choice, without which the very conception of agent makes no sense.

But we are not required to make this difficult choice. It is necessary only if we confuse or identify 'predictable' and 'compelled.' While it is predictable that some will make this error, and even insist upon it, no one is compelled to do so. The contrasted perspectives are indeed different, but they are not incompatible with each other. The question is only about which is relevant, and that depends upon our concerns. But there need be no life and death struggle between students of political behavior and students of political obligation based on a mistaken assumption that the success of one destroys the basis of the other.

Second, the distinction between these two perspectives implies a more limited role for social science than is sometimes suggested by reference to the social sciences as the 'policy sciences.' To the extent that social scientists discipline themselves into purely descriptive and predictive activity—for the sake of being 'behavioral' or 'scientific'—social science, while relevant, leaves the decision-maker without guidance at crucial points in his activity. The art or the training of the decision-maker is not simply identical with that of the social scientist; and a school of government cannot simply be a division of social science.

Third, following from this it seems clear that in the education of the ruler, the political agent, the manner of the tribunal, the relevant perspective is not the descriptive-predictive but rather the normative-practical one. Liberal education is education for the life of action and decision. That action takes place within the decision-making tribunal. Those who man the tribunal must become sensitive to its demands and be prepared to meet them.

The study of the political decision-making process moves, then, in two directions: toward a theory of political behavior—a set of descriptive and predictive hypotheses; and toward a theory of political obligation—an attempt at the delineation of the demands of the political role and of propriety in response to those demands, obligations, or duties. A theory of political obligation is an attempt to provide the elements of an answer to the political agent's 'what should I do?'.

The attempt to take a theory of political obligation as seriously as it deserves is hindered by some characteristic features of our moral and intellectual climate. We like to consider ourselves tough-minded and realistic; we want to discover how things really are, how they work. We prefer the 'is' to the 'ought'—the study of 'what is the case,' to tender-minded speculation about 'what should be.' And we have fallen into the habit of stating the descriptive-normative contrast in these misleading terms—contrasting 'what is' and 'what should be.' The former we reserve for science; the latter we relegate to dreamers, poets, and others notoriously out of touch with the facts of life.

But this is to misunderstand the descriptive-normative distinction. It does not contrast 'what is the case?' with 'what should be?'. It does contrast 'what is the case?' with 'what should be done?'—the concern with knowing and the concern with doing, the spectator and the agent or participant.

Thus, a theory of political obligation, normative though it be, is a response to the demands of the life of action and never strays too far from the quandaries of decision. Concern for the normative is not a speculative luxury; it is a practical necessity.

But our contemporary mood involves more than the suspicion of the normative, and I turn to consider briefly several pairs of contrasting notions toward which we display a troublesome and deep-seated ambivalence.

Risking repetition, I insist that the distinction between power and authority is vital to the understanding of the political enterprise. But this distinction is constantly endangered by the charms of power which we so much prefer to study and to which we often seek to reduce the notion of authority. Power seems so much more substantial than authority and so much more congenial to realists.

Nevertheless, besides the structure of power or influence there is, in the body politic, an intricate web of relations which we describe in such terms as authorization, delegation, constitutionality, rights, duties, and obligations. This may seem a rather insubstantial network; but it is not the ghost, it is the Hamlet of the play. It seems strange that it should be necessary to defend its significance for the understanding of our political life when it is precisely its absence or weakness which constitutes, when we look at other, 'unfree' societies, a chief basis of our condemnation.

Power and authority are not identical and we express our awareness of this in many ways. Might, we say, is not Right. Power can be seized, but *de facto* is not *de jure*. A tyrant exercises power beyond authority; and one who acts *ultra vires* exceeds his authority not his power. Typical political questions—the authority of the President to take over steel mills, the right of Congress to investigate in certain ways, the duty of courts to defend civil rights—these are not questions of mere power. Nor are they settled as easily.

To insist that power and authority are distinct is, of course, not to say they are unrelated. It may be argued, as Hobbes does, that the structure of authority is dissolved if the sovereign becomes powerless to keep the peace. A right may be violated and still be a right, but systematic non-enforcement may bring its status as a right into question. One may wield power without authority or remain impotent with authority. Obviously, power and authority are related in many ways. But they are distinct and irreducible.

For a theory of political obligation and for the education of the political agent the crucial focus is upon authority. It is hard to see what proper political education is if it is not the attempt to make the agent responsive to the demands of the structure of authority within which he is to act. It would be irresponsible folly to teach wielders of authority merely the arts of power.

One of the fruits of the spirit of individualism is the tendency, when we think of the individual, to see him chiefly as a complex of values, desires, drives, or interests. It seems natural for him to pursue his interests, to try to satisfy his desires, to seek to enhance his own 'life-space.' Often we seem to mean by 'respect for the individual' a sympathetic understanding of this situation, a recognition of the legitimacy of the pursuit of one's own good, and a reluctance to impose any unnecessary restraints.

Against this background, attempts to push the claims of duty and obligation have been greeted with deep suspicion and hostility. They seem unnatural demands which involve the disciplining of the individual to the point where he finds himself acting contrary to his own interests, used for some purpose other than his own. And notwithstanding a tradition within which this is not an altogether alien element, the claims of the state are acknowledged with reluctance. That they are acknowledged, however, is evidenced by the indignation we feel when a public trust is betrayed by self-interest. The public agent is expected to do his duty.

At the heart of political life there is thus an inescapable tension between interest and duty, between the inclinations of the private life and the obligations of the public role. Attempts to resolve the tension from either direction are failures. On the one hand, attempts to absorb the individual into his public role so that there is no recalcitrant remainder founder on the fact that man is, after all, an animal, a striving biological organism with a particular identity. No matter how 'social' or 'mature' or 'integrated' he may be he cannot abolish the difference between the immediate and the remote, the particular and the general, 'my own' and 'theirs' or even 'ours.' No theory about the identity of individual and social can quite conceal the difference. Similarly, attempts to dissolve the public role and its demands into the private individual and his interests do not survive much exposure to the plain facts of social life. The conflict between interest and obligation cannot be conjured away; political life will always involve us in moral dilemmas.

While I do not want to ride the theme of 'individualism' too hard its tendency is to exalt interest over duty and obligation. Duty must justify itself at the bar of interest. A public role is not taken for granted as 'natural.' Instead, it poses the question 'why should I, an individual with interests of my own, take on the obligations of a public role which may make demands running counter to my interests?'. This is a question with which a theory of political obligation should deal. But this is easier said than done.

In passing, a word about obligation and freedom. In one of its senses 'to be obliged' is roughly synonymous with 'to be compelled' or 'to be forced.' We say, 'he was obliged to surrender' or 'he was obliged to drop out of the race.' This usage is appropriate in situations in which an option disappears, in which no choice is left. In another sense we speak of 'having an obligation,' as when we say that 'one has an obligation to pay his debts.' It is here supposed that there is a choice, that it is possible to meet or not to meet the obligation. We sometimes distinguish this sort of obligation as 'moral' precisely to indicate that it is not a matter of constraint.

The important difference is that while in the first sense 'being obliged' is incompatible with 'being free,' in the second sense 'being free' is a necessary condition of 'having an obligation.' In its ultimate bearing on the problems of political freedom it is important to remember that only a free man can have obligations and, conversely, that having obligations is not incompatible with freedom.

I have touched briefly on two of the sets of contrasting notions—authority and power, obligation and interest—with which political theory must deal. I turn now, in the same preliminary way, to a third contrast, that between 'public' and 'private.'

Here again we are characteristically ambivalent. We are insistent on the distinction as we jealously protect a private sphere against governmental intrusion. 'This is a private matter,' we say, 'and therefore not the concern of public authority.' We criticize and condemn as 'totalitarian' any political system which fails to distinguish the public from the private.

But we also, at times, seem determined to deny the significance of the distinction, especially in dealing with the relation of public to private interest. However much rhetorical deference we pay to the public interest we try in various ways to by-pass its direct consideration. We dismiss it as 'unknowable,' or as the automatic resultant of private striving after private goods. Almost anything will do so long as we are relieved of worrying about it and allowed to pursue our private interests with a sense of virtue. We even play with the notion that they are identical if only the private interest is 'enlightened,' or 'long-range,' or even 'real.' These efforts, whether adequate or not, bespeak an uneasiness about the public interest, a fear that the individual may be improperly imposed upon, a fear, even, of undemocratic or 'elitist' implications. In spite of the difficulties, and even dangers, the distinction between public and private interest is necessary and crucial.

A moment ago I stressed the gap between the individual's interests and his obligations. I wish now to suggest that obligation and interest may move closer together in a special way. That is, the obligation of a public agent may well be defined in terms of the *public* interest. Thus, for a public agent 'I have an obligation to do X' and 'X is required for the public interest' may be equivalent. But ordinarily 'X is in my interest' and 'I have an obligation to do X' are not equivalent. In other words, the distinction between *public* and *private* may help bridge the gap between *interest* and *obligation*.

There is another aspect of the public-private distinction to which I shall refer briefly. The democratic citizen has a twofold relation to government. In one relation he is a subject, a private person under the law; in the other relation he is a public person, a part of the sovereign tribunal, a maker of the law. It is precisely this combination of private status and public status in every person which distinguishes a system of self-government from any aristocratic polity in which most men are subjects only. This dual status is the source of much confusion, but it is also the key to an understanding of much that is crucial to the theory and practice of democracy.

There is a deadly ambiguity in 'The People'—whose voice is sometimes defied, sometimes deified. In one sense it refers simply to an aggregate or collection of private persons and its voice is only the murmur of private tongues. But in another sense 'The People' is an organization of persons, a group of colleagues manning the sovereign public tribunal, acting in a corporate capacity. There is a world of difference. When we forget it, as we often do, we lose our grasp of the radical distinction between consumer sovereignty and self-government, and acquiesce in a usurpation which may well, I fear, prove fatal to the prospects of democracy.

The central argument here has been that the necessary task of political education requires the development of a theory of political obligation distinct from a theory of political behavior; that a theory which meets the demands of a body politic concerned with political freedom finds the model of the voluntary organization most congenial, or even necessary; and that such a theory must deal seriously and hospitably with concepts which, in our present climate of opinion, are regarded generally with suspicion or hostility.

The current state of political education does not justify much complacency. Nor do I see much prospect of improvement except as we attempt to achieve greater clarity about the elements of political obligation out of which that education must be developed. In this attempt two fundamental concepts present themselves for analysis—*membership* and *agency*. In the neighborhood of these concepts we encounter most of the traditional problems of political theory. But as we deal with them we will, I hope, remember that what we are seeking is always a part of the answer to 'what should I do?' asked in the context of political life.

2

The Member

'The consent of the governed' is an expression laden with significance for political life, but its apparent simplicity conceals many difficulties. Its meaning is not exhausted by saying that the ship of state floats on a sea of popular sentiment, that suffering and acquiescence have limits, that government cannot be both intolerable and enduring. For we are also told that governments derive 'their just powers from the consent of the governed,' and this reminds us of the relation between consent and legitimacy. Consent has not always been regarded as a necessary basis for the claim to political authority, but for the last three hundred years every other basis has been so badly shaken that there is hardly a government which does not claim, however fraudulently, to rest upon it.

There are two aspects of this fundamental consent which traditionally have been distinguished. First, the demand for consent is the demand that the government must be more than self-appointed and must, in some significant way, be the chosen instrument through which the body politic or community acts; the ruler, in short, must be authorized by the ruled. And second, the demand for consent is the demand that membership be distinguishable from captivity. It must in some meaningful sense be voluntary.

The fact that consent is sometimes discussed with reference to the relation of government to the body politic and at other times with reference to the relation of the individual to the body politic is itself a cause of some confusion and controversy. Thus it is possible to hold that membership in a body politic is not voluntary but that the demand for consent is satisfied if the government is authorized by some consent-giving process. It may also be held that government need not be authorized but that the demand for consent is satisfied if membership in the body politic is voluntarily acquired and voluntarily relinquishable. And it may, of course, be insisted that consent is lacking unless membership is voluntary *and* the government is properly authorized.

The possibility of thus distinguishing voluntary adherence from the authorization of government has led theorists to distinguish between a 'pact of association' and a 'pact of government'—the former, an agreement which transforms a multitude or aggregate of individuals into a single community or organization; the latter, an agreement by which the community establishes its government. But to separate distinguishable aspects into two distinct acts is not only to multiply entities needlessly, it is to obscure the whole point. The act which creates a body politic out of a multitude is precisely the act by which a number of individuals establish a common decision-making authority; the act by which one acquires membership is the act of accepting the authority of the government. Thus, for example, the ratification of the Constitution which created our Federal Union involved for each state the acceptance of the authority of the proposed government. That single act created both a new body politic and the new governing authority. The agreement which makes one a member is the agreement to be governed in a particular way.

It is easy to forget that the consent of the governed, upon which we insist, is consent to be governed. If it is a voluntary act it is nevertheless an act of voluntary subordination. A body politic is not a state of anarchy in which sovereign individuals confront each other; it is an organization in which individuals are sovereign neither in theory nor in practice but are related as members or parts of a system. The consent which is seen as the necessary basis of a body politic is precisely the acceptance by the individual of the status of 'member.' And this involves a significant twofold subordination.

The first aspect of subordination is that by which one acknowledges himself bound by a decision other than his own—the subordination of private judgment to public judgment. This may sound rather offensive to our independent ears, but it is really one of the most familiar features of political life.

Consider, for example, a political caucus. A number of individuals faced with the necessity for agreement upon a concerted course of action bind themselves to act upon the decision of the caucus, determined, let us suppose, by a majority vote. This is done with full awareness that participation in the caucus involves binding oneself to act upon a decision which one may, in fact, vote against. To enter a caucus is thus to acknowledge the authority of a decision other than one's own. It is obvious that adhering to or being a member of a caucus is a matter of voluntary decision, that *every* member is a party to the caucus agreement, that no one would be considered a member who would insist on a veto power, thus claiming to be bound only by a decision with which he agrees, and that no one is bound by the decision who is not a member of the caucus or at least represented at it.

It is generally assumed or expected that the caucus decision will not be unanimous; for if unanimity is required the caucus agreement is pointless. It is precisely the failure of unanimity which makes the caucus necessary. There is thus both a presupposition of unanimity and a deliberate rejection of the demand for unanimity. The sense in which unanimity is presupposed is the sense in which everyone who is a member is a party to the agreement. But the unanimous agreement is to the bindingness of subsequent non-unanimous decisions and, in this form, to the subordination of individual judgment to group judgment and decision.

The real problem is that of getting away from the demand for unanimity as a condition of group action. This requires creating a situation in which the 'group' can be said to decide or to act not only in the face of non-concurrence by a portion of its members but with the understanding that the dissenters are bound to consider the decision as *theirs*. The voice of the majority, for example, is designated as the voice of the group. But this designation must be by each member, since there is nothing inherently authoritative about a majority. We are sometimes so impressed with the democratic aspect of majority rule that we forget that it does involve some abdication of autonomy and the subordination of private decision to the decision of the group. Without this subordination there would, in fact, be no caucus. To be a member is thus to subordinate oneself.

What is so dramatically apparent in the caucus, the unanimous agreement to transcend the demand for unanimity, is

an essential feature of any situation in which voting is significantly involved. It may, in fact, be said to be the crucial
invention of the political mind. We are so familiar with it
that, as with the wheel, we seldom think of it as an achievement. But where would we be without it? How much concerted, group action would there be if we always needed
unanimity? Considering this, it is hardly surprising that
the agreement to waive unanimity should come to be regarded as *the* social compact.

Whether it be described as the delegation of decision-
making authority or the authorization of a decision-making
tribunal or the acceptance of the jurisdiction of a tribunal,
what is involved is the voluntary waiving of autonomy, the
voluntary subordination of private to public decision. 'To
delegate,' 'to authorize,' 'to put oneself under the jurisdiction of' are, of necessity, voluntary acts; they are ways of
giving consent. But its voluntary character must not obscure
the hard fact that it is an act of subordination, giving precedence to public over private decision. A body politic,
based on consent, is a group of individuals each of whom is
a party to a basic agreement, making a common delegation
of authority, acknowledging, within its proper scope, the
the subordination of private to public decision.

This is not the whole story. The act of subordination is
not pointless or unbounded. It is a purposive act, and its
purposive character brings us to another aspect of the subordination involved in membership—the subordination of
private to public purpose.

Familiar as it is, there is something fundamentally misleading about the slogan that the aim of government is
'the welfare of the individual.' It is hard to quarrel with the
demand that the body politic provide or safeguard the conditions necessary for the fullest development of each of its

members. And I do not intend to quarrel with it. But I do not think we can escape the distinction between the demands or interests of a particular individual and the demands of the system of interests of which any individual's is only a part. The government's concern is, and must be, systemic. If it deals with some individual or individuals with hostility we condemn its action as discriminatory; if it treats some with special softness we accuse it of partiality. This recognition of the impropriety of discrimination and partiality testifies to the fact that the government's concern for the individual is not to be understood as special concern for *this* or *that* individual but rather as concern for all individuals. Government, that is to say, serves the welfare of the community. And if it be said here that the 'welfare of the community' means simply the welfare of the individuals who constitute it, that the general good is simply the sum of particular goods, the point still holds. For there is a very real difference between trying to maximize my private good and trying to maximize the whole system of private goods—as any Utilitarian faced with a pack of Hedonists will quickly realize. Even in individualistic terms, then, the distinction between a particular interest and the system, or complex, or collection of particular interests forces itself upon us in a way which requires us to state the government's concern as with the general or public good, with *ours* rather than with *mine*.

If, then, the agreement which constitutes a body politic involves the subordination of private judgment to public judgment, and if the public judgment is directed at the public interest, there is also a significant subordination of private interest to public interest. To be a member is to acknowledge that one's own interests are only a part of a broader system of interests, that other members have theirs as you have yours, and that it is the function of government to promote and safeguard the entire system, of which yours is a part but no more significant a part than any other's.

To see membership as based on consent is to regard this subordination as voluntary. And here we encounter a familiar difficulty. Why should I, the guardian of my own interests, subordinate these interests to other interests and meekly accept the status of a part? Does it help much to say that the question itself is a symptom of moral disorder and really should not be asked? Is it really an answer to say that this subordination is not subordination at all but is simply getting the most one can in an imperfect world? Are we satisfied with the answer that accepting this subordination is what 'being moral' or 'being a good citizen' really *means*. Questions queue up behind each tentative answer, but we can at least suggest that the voluntary character of membership in a body politic involves: (1) some justification for the subordination in the light of the interests and purposes of the individual, (2) recognition of some *common* or shared concern, and (3) some recognition that one's own interests constitute only a subordinate part of a broader system of interests.

The twofold subordination involved in membership in a body politic is, I have argued, that of private to public decision and private to public interest or purpose. This duality is the source of an interesting and persistent tension in political life. We are committed to public purposes or ends. We are also committed to authoritative decision-making procedures. And we are at times torn in different directions. A decision may seem to us to flout a fundamental purpose and we are tempted to fly to purpose in an appeal from decision. We are then reminded of the anarchy that would ensue if everyone reserved the right of private veto and, abandoning our claim, defer to the judgment other than our own by which we have agreed to act. In doing so we come to regard the commitment to means or procedures as an end in itself. We rhapsodize about and glorify 'the process' which, as it looms larger, grows emptier and directionless as public purpose is displaced. A process without a dominating purpose is an invitation hard to resist. Our private interests swarm in; the forum becomes first an arena, then a marketplace; the public decision becomes a bargain; the 'process' degenerates into compromise; and we are left singing the praises of the public spirit over its corpse.

The harshness of subordination is in some measure mitigated by the fact that the membership it creates carries with it a claim to an important range of rights, to which, apart from that status, one might have no valid claim. The two aspects of subordination are matched by two fundamental rights which, in our own tradition, are expressed as the right to 'equal protection' and the right to 'due process.' The former seems to soften the subordination of private to public interest by asserting the equal claim of each private person to public consideration, by denying that there are first-class and second-class citizens, by forbidding discrimination or special favor. While we are far from realizing this fundamental demand completely or adequately in our political life, our failure is at least recognized as failure and as unfinished business. The claim to due process, on the other hand, qualifies the subordination to public decision by the demand that such decision must be 'appropriately' reached and should not be 'unreasonable' or 'arbitrary.' The history and effectiveness of this demand is a long and interesting story—as every student of government knows—but I shall not attempt to tell it here.

Beyond these are other rights, tied more closely to the character of the particular political or legal order—the rights created or bestowed or, on some views, recognized by law. Some of these may be regarded as more important or fundamental than others and their denial felt as a violation of the demands of 'morality' as well as 'legality.' Other rights created by law may seem less important, and when a member is deprived of such a right we may feel that the deprivation is a fact of greater significance than the right itself. It is clear that, while rights are rights, they are not usually regarded as equally important.

I leave out of account here an important class of rights, or 'liberties,' sometimes described as 'civil' or 'political,' generally associated with participation in political life or activity. I do so because I follow Alexander Meiklejohn in distinguishing between the rights we have as subjects or members and the rights we have as rulers or agents, and I am concerned here only with the former. Whether every person who is a member of a body politic should also be regarded as having the right to participate in the public decision-making process is a question for which democratic theory has its distinctive answer.

To be a member of a body politic is thus to be a voluntary ✓ party to a basic agreement or system of agreements which involves the subordination of private to public interest and of private to public decision and which establishes a claim to a broad range of rights. It is difficult to see how one could claim the rights without having made the subordination or how one can be held to the subordination and denied the rights. Both are inseparable aspects of membership.

This phase of the discussion cannot end without a word about what inevitably comes to mind when we think of subordination or the duty of obedience. What about the limits of obedience? What of the right to disobey or even the right to revolt? I attempt to deal with these questions below, but it should be said here that they presuppose a theory of obedience. There can be a right to disobey only if there is first a duty to obey; there can be a right to revolt only if there is also a duty to support. If this seems paradoxical it is less so than the view that there is a limit to obedience without a duty to obey. The limit of obedience is the fringe of the garment of obligation.

The Acceptance of Membership

The assertion that the citizen or member of a body politic is a party to a system of agreements inevitably evokes the surprised response—'when did I agree to any such thing?'. In an age of oaths I would hesitate to suggest another, but I cannot help thinking how much simpler political theory would be at this point if we had the equivalent of the Ephebic Oath embedded in a ceremonial secular confirmation service reminding the native citizen that he, too, shares the commitment or agreement which is quite explicit in the case of the naturalized citizen. In its absence my path is a wearier and harder one.

What is at stake is the question of the 'social compact' as an historic fact. Are we, as citizens, in fact parties to a basic agreement? Can our relations to each other, to the body politic, be properly described in such terms? The answer is yes—with qualifications, unfortunately. The basic agreement is not simply a myth or fiction, nor even an 'ideal,' although it is also that, but is in fact an actually existing condition which cannot be ignored in any description of

our political relatedness without reducing to meaningless-
ness what we most value.

It is quite easy to ridicule the ridiculous notion of an
original or aboriginal contract by which a collection of sav-
ages solemnly and at one stroke, tiring of the state of nature,
invent civilization. This is not only a dead horse, it is an
imaginary dead horse. But there is a real 'historical' question
and we meet it in two forms. The difference is roughly the
difference between becoming a charter member and becoming a member of a going concern, between forming a
body politic and joining an already existing body politic.
While I am chiefly concerned with the latter, the former
should not be dismissed without a brief remark.

We are not unfamiliar with the process of creating a
new body politic by explicit agreement. How else are we
to describe the process of promulgating and ratifying the
Constitution which created our Federal Union? A more
recent example is the creation of the United Nations which,
while lacking some of the necessary conditions of being a
body politic, has some of its features. There is nothing in
the discussions of the last decade about the United Nations
which would be in the slightest degree strange or novel to
Hobbes—sovereignty and veto power, enforcement problems, rights and duties under the charter, reservations about
self-preservation, fear of mutual destruction—the whole
story. It is of no special significance that the units involved
are themselves states. The problem is that of creating a
system of agreements, to which states are voluntary parties,
with decision-making tribunals authorized to deal effec-
tively with the problems whose existence makes the organization necessary. In this area we still move entirely
within the basic analysis and concepts of social contract
theory.

It should be noted that both the United States and the United Nations have members who are not charter members—who were not in on the formation of the organization—but who have become members of a going concern by becoming parties to the same system of agreements. Too much attention is given to the original agreement and not enough to the process by which one becomes a member of an already existing body politic. This is the form in which the question 'when did I agree?' presents itself to us.

Let us first consider the case of the person, not born a citizen of the United States, who, through the process of naturalization, becomes a member of the body politic in full standing. At the threshold of citizenship he is called upon to give and does give his explicit 'consent.' He agrees to recognize the authority of the governing institutions, the constitution, and the laws made pursuant to it. He makes his submission, pledges his allegiance, and is received as a member with the rights which go with that status. He is not required to 'agree' with every existing law. There may be laws in force which he might well have opposed had he had a voice in the matter and which he would like to have a hand in changing. But he acknowledges the authority of the whole system. In giving his consent he declares himself a party to the system of agreements which constitute the body politic.

For the naturalized citizen, therefore, the question 'when did I agree?' has a clear and easy answer. At a particular time and place he gave his express consent. But for the native citizen the problem seems more difficult. We commonly distinguish the minor from the adult citizen, but we seem to drift or grow into full citizenship without ceremony. Yet I wonder if we would really consider the difference between the naturalized and native citizen as the difference between one who has 'consented' and one who has not. We do sometimes speak of the one as a citizen 'by choice,' but do we mean by this to indicate that only the naturalized are governed by consent? I think not. We fall back rather, upon the familiar notion of tacit consent.

There are many occasions upon which the native citizen makes a formal, ceremonial pledge which could well be regarded as an express giving of consent. I mention this but I do not depend on it. I am intrigued, however, by the baffled and puzzled reaction of many persons when this is called to their attention and by their resistance to the suggestion that they have, in this form, 'consented.' Perhaps this attitude is the result of making the pledge of allegiance a schoolboy ritual, robbing it of any moral significance; perhaps it is a symptom of something even more disturbing. But I leave this matter unexplored and turn to the question of tacit consent.

The difference between express and tacit consent is not, I think, the difference between two kinds or degrees of consent. It is a difference in the way in which consent is given. There is really little point in insisting that the only way in which consent can be indicated or given is by the express utterance of 'I consent' or 'I pledge allegiance.' Not only may there be other verbal acts which can be interpreted as the giving of consent, but there may be non-verbal acts which have the same force. So that the question of tacit consent is the question of whether there are some actions, including perhaps, the failure to act, which can properly be regarded as the equivalent of the express consent given by the naturalized citizen.

That there are such acts has been the traditional view. Voting, for example, has generally been regarded as implying consent or allegiance; as has applying for a passport. It is not profitable, however, to argue abstractly about the acts which can be taken as a sign that one has become a party to the system of agreements constituting a body politic. Beyond insisting that there is little justification for the narrow demand that nothing but the signature on the dotted line will serve, there is one crucial point that needs to be made.

There is a necessary condition which must be satisfied *whatever* is proposed as a sign of tacit consent. That is, the act can only be properly taken as 'consent' if it is done 'knowingly,' if it is understood by the one performing the act that his action involves his acceptance of the obligations of membership. This condition seems to me so crucial that, in fact, it may even override the force of an explicit verbal expression of consent. That is why we take the child's pledge lightly. He says the magic words, but he does not know quite what he is saying. It is form without substance.

While this may involve complications, we cannot really regard 'entrapment' as possible here—as when a man performs a particular act and subsequently has it held up to him as evidence that he has agreed or consented and is thus caught in bonds he knew nothing of. Consent must be voluntary, not unconscious or accidental. We take good care that in naturalization the knowing quality of the act is preserved. Unfortunately we do not do as well with the native, and this is a grave failure in political education. It has disturbing consequences.

When we reflect upon what we mean when we describe ourselves as members of a body politic I think we come to accept the fact that it means we have agreed to something, that we are parties to a social compact. But we must accept it as a plain fact that many native 'citizens' have in no meaningful sense agreed to anything. They have never been asked and have never thought about it. They are political child-brides who have a status they do not understand and which they have not acquired by their own consent.

If it is true that 'American Citizen' includes some who have 'agreed' and some who have not, we seem to be in some difficulty. If it is insisted that only those who have consented are members of the body politic then the body politic may shrink alarmingly. But if all—those who have not consented as well as those who have—are regarded as members, then consent cannot be taken as a necessary condition of membership.

Confronted with these alternatives I conclude, with some reluctance, that some variant of the 'shrinkage' notion needs to be accepted. Or rather, it must be recognized that the class of minors, or others who for some reason are regarded as lacking full status, is larger than we think. Any description of a body politic, like the United States, would have to recognize that there are some, or many, 'citizens' who could not be described as having consented. There is no point to resorting to fiction to conceal this fact. It makes more sense to speak of the social compact as an ideal which is never completely realized. Non-consenting adult citizens are, in effect, like minors who are governed without their own consent. The period of tutelage and dependence is unduly prolonged. And this, as I have suggested earlier, is a failure of political education.

Something should be said about the voluntary character of the act of becoming a party to the basic agreement. I have already spoken of its 'knowing' character. But it is sometimes said that membership is not voluntary because there is no real choice, no alternative to giving one's consent. We cannot, of course, have it both ways: we cannot assert on the one hand that government is based on consent, and on the other hand that membership, and the subordination it entails, is involuntary.

Only if we suppose that an act which is motivated is, therefore, involuntary is there any real difficulty; but this is to confuse reasonable with involuntary acts. Of course there are reasons for giving one's consent, and very good ones. But to have good reasons is not to be compelled or to have no alternative; it does not rob a deliberate choice of its voluntary character. There is a difference between an alternative's being inconvenient, hard, or unpleasant and its being impossible. The fact that the easier course is easier does not make the harder course impossible. There is considerable range before we come to the situation in which choice disappears because an alternative is really no alternative at all. 'Your money or your life!' may not really present you with a choice; but to say that consenting to the status of a member is involuntary because the alternative is not as pleasant or convenient is simply to confuse convenience with necessity. And if we have come to the point at which we find the inconvenient really impossible then we are beyond the help of political or moral theory and in need of psychiatric treatment. Difficult as the alternative to citizenship may be, there is sufficient alternative to preserve the voluntary character of the consent which creates membership.

To the extent that 'becoming a member' of a body politic involves the express or tacit giving of the consent by which one becomes a party to the agreements which constitute a structure of authority, the conception of the body politic as a voluntary group finds its embodiment in the real world. To this extent is it possible to speak meaningfully of government based on the consent of the governed. We must ask ourselves, then, whether it is not the case that we, as citizens, native as well as naturalized, have agreed to something. We must ask ourselves, when we claim to be free men, whether we are not asserting that we are voluntary parties to the social compact.

WITHDRAWAL AND REJECTION

The severance of the political bond has seemed a solemn enough matter to require unusual justification. In our brief history we have had occasion to fight to dissolve such bonds and to fight to prevent a dissolution of an indissoluble union. At the individual level we have long proclaimed the right to quit one body politic to join a different one—a position quite natural for a country built by immigration. In this whole unsettled area we see a conflict between the conception of permanence rooted in pre-consent theories of membership and the idea of consent-based joining and quitting demanded by an epoch of mobility and political change.

There seems to be nothing inherently contradictory in the notion of a voluntary commitment which is also permanent. Nevertheless, it seems to enhance the quality of freedom in our membership if, in addition to its being voluntarily entered into, there is a continuing option of withdrawal; consent in this circumstance seems constantly renewed rather than merely once given. And this, as well as other practical considerations, supports the demand for the possibility of disengagement.

If the right to withdraw is conceded there are still some qualifications which should be observed. The right to withdraw may not be available as a device for avoiding obligations or for escaping, so to speak, the luck of the draw. Suppose, for example, that a group of men in a perilous situation agrees that one of them must run a risk and that the risk-taker shall be chosen by lot. If upon drawing the short straw one claims the right to withdraw, the recognition of that right would frustrate the entire enterprise. At that stage the time for withdrawal has passed, although it might come again. The right to withdraw is limited by considerations of this sort.

It is also appropriate to protect the status of membership against impulse by requiring that the act of withdrawal be deliberate or cool and not under stress or in unconsidered haste. While this may be a question of degree, there is some point to distinguishing between decision, or resolution, and impulse; government is full of devices by which we try to protect our basic resolves against our transient moods; we need cooling-off periods. To use a homely analogy, the dieter who resolves to forgo sweets may be overcome by craving and break his resolution; but we would hesitate to say he had changed his mind or revoked his decision.

It was the recognition of some such distinction which led the Supreme Court to hold that the 'renunciation' of American citizenship by American citizens of Japanese ancestry confined to 'camps' during World War II did not really constitute renunciation.

Thus, while the right of an individual to withdraw from a body politic is generally recognized, it is subject to some limitations designed to protect the integrity of both the body politic and the individual.

But what of the right of the body politic, or the government, to divest a person of his membership without his consent, to excommunicate, denationalize, or expatriate? This is a question which today finds our Supreme Court closely and deeply divided. *Perez* v. *Brownell* and *Trop* v. *Dulles*, decided during the 1957 term, are fascinating not only as dealing with this problem but also as a striking example of the involvement of the Court in political theory. Denationalization as *punishment* has been held to be 'cruel and unusual' by the same Court, slightly realigned, which upheld, on the ground of possible avoidance of embarrassment to the government in the conduct of foreign affairs, the denationalization of one who voted in a foreign election.

The problem is a complicated one. It seems strange to hold that there is nothing a person may do which forfeits his status as a member, even though he may forfeit by his acts, his liberty or his life, or may, by his own decision, withdraw. On the other hand, I think we are uneasy at the prospect of the body politic acting on the biblical view that if a part offend (or embarrass) you, throw it out.

It might be instructive to try to discover the assumptions underlying the quite different attitude we take about the right of a state to withdraw or secede from the Federal Union. We seem, since the Civil War at least, to regard this as out of the question. But elsewhere political units of larger political organizations withdraw or consider withdrawal and, as often as not, the claim of a right to withdraw evokes our unshocked sympathy. Is ours a uniquely eternal and indissoluble union? This is hardly a pressing question now, but when we have fifty-three or sixty-one states—and whoever thought that there would be more than forty-eight—we may find the question of withdrawal a perfectly reasonable one and may need to re-examine the 'indissolubility' of union.

DISOBEDIENCE AND REBELLION

Membership involves the delegation of authority; and the other side of delegation is obedience. If authority is limited so is the obligation to obey. The question is whether the authority of government is 'absolute' or whether it is meaningful to speak of government exceeding or abusing its authority.

It is intrinsic to the concept of authority that, however great it may be, it can be overstepped or abused. 'Absolute' authority, the authority to do anything whatever in any manner whatsoever, is complete license. To claim it is to claim irresponsibility. But to have authority is to have responsibility. 'Absolute' authority is an absurdity.

It is interesting to consider, in this connection, the familiar expression—'The King can do no wrong.' This is often taken to mean that whatever the King may do he has authority to do, that his authority is unlimited. But it is really a paradoxical way of saying that the authority of the King is limited. It assumes the distinction between the 'office' and the 'occupant,' between the official and the natural person, and simply asserts that the drunken acts of Philip are not the authoritative acts of Philip sober. The 'wrong' act is not the act of the King but of his private companion. This distinction, odd or trivial as it may sound to the uninitiated, has considerable practical significance beyond that of the relation of the King's 'two bodies.' It is involved, for example, in the question of who is responsible and who can be sued when a public officer exceeds the authority of his office.

Authority, I shall assume, is limited; it is possible that

it may be abused or exceeded by its wielders. The claim that authority has been exceeded usually takes one of three familiar forms.

First, it may be held that the wielder of authority is frustrating or ignoring the purpose for which the authority has been granted. This is seldom a clear or easy matter, but the distinction between proper and improper purpose is built into the conception of a purposive delegation of authority and provides a basis for challenge.

Second, an act may be challenged on grounds of arbitrariness, as lacking in procedural propriety, or even as so failing in wisdom as to fall outside the range of permissible folly. This, too, is vague; but authority is limited by such considerations.

And third, 'higher law' doctrines confront the exercise of authority with the assertion that there are rules or principles or 'rights' which are impervious to the demands of political authority and which mark its limits.

I take it as beyond argument that, in principle, the member has an obligation to obey only the 'authorized' actions of public authority. *Ultra vires* acts have no valid claim upon him, although they certainly put him in a quandary. Disobedience or revolt even when justified are not light undertakings and, if justified, mark a failure in the structure of authority.

It is useful to distinguish disobedience and revolt, although they have something in common. A situation may sometimes justify disobedience when it would not justify revolution. The distinction I suggest is between a situation in which the general structure of authority is unimpaired and a situation in which the bonds of authority and obligation are dissolved. Or perhaps it can be put this way: Disobedience is justified if there is still a 'healthy' tribunal to which appeal can be made; rebellion, when there is not. Vague as it is, this distinction captures the point that disobedience is usually the initiation of an appeal, while the right to revolt is peculiar as a 'right' precisely because it is not urged before a tribunal but rather marks the abandonment of hope in tribunal remedies.

To acknowledge the possibility that the acts of public officers may exceed governmental authority requires the recognition of occasions of justified disobedience by members. But at what point it becomes proper to revolt is, of course, hard to say. Some patience seems called for, some attempt to 'exhaust the remedies,' before the appeal is to heaven. The Declaration of Independence speaks of 'a history of repeated injuries and usurpations, all having in direct object the establishment of an absolute tyranny . . .' In the face of tyrannical intention what else is there to do? Appeal again to the tyrant?

These considerations are, of course, relevant only to disobedience or revolt against a government claiming authority based on consent. Where government is based on force, forceful opposition needs no special permit, and war is simply a continuation of 'politics' by other means.

The irritating vagueness of this discussion points up the force of the question 'who is to judge?'. Who is to judge whether government has exceeded its authority in a particular case or when it has evidenced tyrannical intention? There have been two general answers, neither of which seems entirely satisfactory. There is the view that government itself is the judge of whether it has overstepped the limits of its authority. And there is the opposed view that the subject is the judge of whether government is making a legitimate demand upon him. The first seems to increase

the danger of tyranny, while the second poses the threat of
anarchy.

Let me put the question again in these familiar terms.
Who is to judge whether an act of government is 'constitutional'? Congress has broad, but limited, authority. It
has sworn to observe its constitutional limits. Should it be
the judge of what those limits preclude or allow? It sometimes says so, and it meets with considerable support when
it does. Is the President the judge of the limits of his constitutional authority? Some great Presidents have thought
so. And the Court, whose own members seem so troubled
by the fact that it is the guardian of the limits of its own
powers? The Court is, after all, a branch of the government
even though we sometimes think of it as a third party, an
arbiter between the government and the subject. Do we all,
and always, accept the Court as the authoritative judge of
constitutionality? When it declares the fugitive-slave law
constitutional? When it declares segregation unconstitutional?

Somewhere, we tend to say, there must be an authoritative judgment about whether an act is constitutional—otherwise there is chaos. And the special place of the Supreme
Court in American life is a reflection of this demand. But
it is a part of government, and even if we try to set it apart
as the special arbiter of constitutionality the acceptance of
its authority involves, for the individual, the abdication of
the final authority of his own judgment—and conscience.

If we recoil from this, to what do we turn? To the conscience of each individual, or the creed of each group, or
the culture of each locality? Not for long, if we want a
national government. To 'The People,' then, as Locke said?
But no one has ever told us clearly how 'The People' acts,

except through its government; and that does not help us here.

The right to disobey and to revolt seems thus to get lost in the question 'who is to judge?' If we answer, 'The Court' (or the government) then disobedience still has its place as putting an appeal in process, but must give way to adverse judgment. The disobeyer is the community's self-appointed test case. But the right to revolt, undeniable in principle, has been buried in this shuffle, as Hobbes buried it. The Court, on this view, takes its place.

But the right of revolution, without a writ, without a forum, still lurks at the outer fringes of political life. It comes to life when government weakens the moral and legitimate basis of its authority. It calls to the aid of the community the moral revolutionist, the self-appointed agent of a body politic betrayed by its appointed agents.

MEMBERSHIP AND LOYALTY

The problem of loyalty has been much with us in recent years, but while we have learned something we have not really won our way through to significant clarity or understanding. We have wearied of some excesses, but we are not much happier over the triumph of our moderation. There is a legitimate demand for loyalty. But 'loyalty' is surrounded by so many dangerous and fraudulent doubles that we are tempted in despair to turn our backs upon the whole business. But common sense sees loyalty as a virtue and demands it, even in its corrupt guise. And thus we find ourselves torn between the undeniable but indiscriminate demand and the troubled rejection of all demands, lest in granting anything we grant too much. Our task is that of clarifying, and embracing, a proper conception of loyalty. Only when we have done this can we fend off its corrupted versions whose embrace threatens to smother the very conception of political freedom and dignity.

Loyalty, at the very least, involves the recognition of something other than the private self or self-interest as an object of devotion. 'I am loyal to myself' is a way of denying loyalty, just as 'I am generous to myself' is a denial of generosity. Loyalty thus confronts hedonic individualism with an interesting challenge. It levies claims against self-interest. And the most common betrayal is at this point. For every betrayal of the 'national interest' out of loyalty to another nation how many times is it betrayed to private interest? This is the treason to which we have become callous.

The demand for loyalty is sometimes seen as a demand for the sentiment of attachment, for a feeling of tribal solidarity, for love of folk or country. It is viewed as 'a matter of the heart.' But what does this ask of us? Are we to like our fellow citizens? All of them? Most of them? More than foreigners? Are we to like American cars, or literature, or music, our cities, our landscape? Are we to be sentimental about our symbols, our flag and anthem, our framed declarations, our founding fathers?

There is, of course, a kernel of significance behind these strange demands. A human enterprise is sustained by human warmth. An enduring institution must be rooted somewhere in feeling. A body politic dies when its members cease to identify themselves with it. If this were not true we could dismiss the identification of loyalty with 'sentiment' without a second thought.

At the same time I am somewhat bemused by the world thus turned upside down. There was a day when we thought that the passions divided men and that a common 'reason' united them. Perhaps the 'thinking reed' has been a slender reed; but can we lean very heavily upon the irenic possibilities of passion and sentiment? Feeling has other objects than the body politic and properly ignores its boundaries. Some of the greatest horrors of our age have been attempts to cut the cloth of feeling to fit the state.

So we shudder when we see them coming—the sentimental loyalists—with the standard props, the banners, slogans, myths, the quick tear for the unread document, the lurking bellicosity, the xenophobic hint. To call this loyalty is to confuse the spirit of the pub with public spirit.

We turn from loyalty as the sentiment of attachment to its companion misconception: loyalty as cognitive concurrence, as agreement in belief. We are not unfamiliar with the spirit which takes orthodoxy as loyalty and which considers disagreement with or criticism or rejection of certain common beliefs as disloyalty. It is this demand for uncritical acceptance which gives to the life of the 'intellectual' its distinctive tension. He is, in one of his functions, the guardian of objectivity against the overwhelming force of familiarity and local common sense. Some, at least, in finding feet of clay among the idols of the tribe, must cry havoc. We should not be surprised if this creates suspicion and alienation.

The question is whether being a loyal member requires refraining from criticism or having certain beliefs. Are there views or positions, the holding of which constitutes disloyalty? We are torn here between adherence to the great tradition of freedom of mind and the recognition that ideas are related to conduct and thus relevant to the undertaking of membership.

It may help to distinguish, tentatively, two classes of beliefs or ideas. First, consider beliefs of this sort: 'We would be better off without free-enterprise'; 'The Constitution is hopelessly inadequate'; 'The first amendment ought to be repealed'; 'Segregation is a better plan than integration'; 'The Russians have as much right to be in the Middle East as we have'; 'The American way of life is silly'; 'The F.B.I. is no better than a Gestapo.' These are controversial statements and they do things to blood pressure. I am not interested here in the correctness of these views but only in whether holding them constitutes disloyalty. And the answer, I think, is 'No.' These are views about our institutions and practices which may be wise or foolish, popular or unpopular. But to hold them does not involve a betrayal of membership.

The second class includes beliefs of this sort: 'It's all right to break the law if you can get away with it'; 'Oaths or promises don't mean a thing'; 'No one has any obligations.' These, too, are controversial statements, but they do not generate as much heat as those in the first class. This is rather surprising since if there *are* beliefs which can be regarded as incompatible with loyal membership they are beliefs of this sort. It would, for example, be outrageous to deny citizenship to an alien because he believed that we would be better off without free enterprise. But what if, before taking his oath of allegiance, he asserted that 'Oaths don't mean a thing and no one has any obligations'?

Little as we may relish this line of argument, there seem to be some beliefs, 'moral' or 'ethical' perhaps, relevant to fitness for membership. In an earlier day this found expression in the requirement that membership in the church was a necessary condition for membership in the body politic, providing the moral basis for political life. We have disestablished the church, but have we freed political life of dependence on morality? Or has the body politic taken over the task of cultivating the morality it needs? And if this includes beliefs about the obligatoriness of agreements is not a moral test appropriate even if a religious test is not? Some such conviction, I think, underlies the widespread tolerance of loyalty oaths and the general bewilderment in the face of fervent, minority opposition.

Perhaps when we are concerned about a belief like 'there is nothing wrong about not keeping agreements' it is not the belief itself that worries us but the fear of what it might lead to. The case of loyalty might be compared with honesty. Do we mean by an honest man one who in practice tells the truth, pays his bills, does not overcharge, etc.? Or do we insist that he is not really honest unless he 'believes in honesty,' and, moveover, believes in it or values it for its own sake. So that if he is honest only because it is the best policy he is not really honest. This is a familiar theme of ethical theory, and I refer to it here only because it reminds us of the tendency sometimes to be concerned with beliefs and motives, sometimes with outward action.

Would it be enough, with respect to loyalty, to regard it as the fulfilling of obligations, whatever the state of mind or motive? The loyal member, then, would be one who does his duty. No doubt we would still distinguish between one who merely does his duty and one who acts out of respect for duty; between one who is merely loyal and one who is 'loyal to loyalty.' But if performance is enough the line is drawn outside the mind, and the demand for loyalty is not the demand for a particular belief or motive. The relevance of belief to action, however, cannot be denied. And to suppose that the body politic has no stake in the cultivation of mind and character is to bury one's head in the sand. Our theory of education is crucial at this point, and I suggest again, as I have elsewhere, that the unifying

theme of public education must be a theory of political
obligation.

I do not see how we can develop an adequate conception
of political loyalty except in terms of the social compact
theory of the state. Beneath the demand for oaths and
probes lies the conviction, however inarticulate, that members of a body politic must share a basic commitment to a
common enterprise, must accept the rules of the game, and
that to reject or betray that commitment constitutes disloyalty. I find it difficult to imagine a rejection of this view
which succeeds in making sense out of the claim to the
rights of membership. But the commitment involved needs
to be carefully understood. It must be kept from degenerating into the demand for sentimental solidarity; it must
be guarded against confusion with the uncritical acceptance
of this or that institution, or belief, which enjoys momentary
orthodoxy. It is failure at these points which leads us to
destroy, with misguided zeal, the conditions which make
loyalty a virtue for free men.

MEMBERSHIP AND FREEDOM

We are frequently reminded that the achievement, and
preservation, of order exacts its price in freedom, that some
freedom must be given up, that we must carefully and
constantly balance the demands of these unfortunately com-
peting goods. To see membership in a body politic as involving subordination heightens the sense of a paradise lost.
The 'consent of the governed' seems rather to mitigate than
to restore, so that political freedom seems to be what is
left after we have paid the unavoidable price.

To the extent that political order and membership in a

body politic do in fact limit freedom the question is whether what we get in exchange is worth the price. I shall not, however, argue the case for civilization over anarchy. I wish rather to consider whether, on several of our ordinary conceptions of freedom, the opposition of freedom to order is quite as clear as it often is taken to be.

First, let us consider freedom as 'doing as one likes.' It seems obvious that if membership imposes obligations and subjects one to the demands and restrictions of law then membership interferes with doing as we like at a great many points. But before jumping to the conclusion that membership, therefore, diminishes our freedom we ought to consider whether it does not in fact so increase the options and possibilities open to us that on any reasonable assessment it increases rather than diminishes the opportunity or power 'to do as one likes.' Anyone who has struggled for a place on a ski lift before a line is established will acknowledge that enforcing the law of the line increases rather than diminishes his power to do as he likes. We chafe at rules ungratefully. Kant somewhere speaks of the dove who, as he flies, bemoans the resistance of the air, thinking how much faster he would go in a vacuum. We should recall this parable in our flighty moments when we berate the rules which make our activity possible. This is, of course, not the whole story, but if we consider its implications membership in a body politic will not necessarily appear as a diminution of freedom.

Second, let us consider freedom as 'governing oneself.' This is not quite the same as 'doing as one likes'; it rests on a different conception of the self and finds expression in Rousseau's 'The mere impulse of appetite is slavery, while obedience to a law which we prescribe to ourselves is liberty.' On this view the question of freedom turns not on the freedom of desire from regulation but on the self-imposed character of that regulation. We are free when we are self-governing, making and following our own rules. And it appears to be more difficult to reconcile membership with this conception of freedom than with the one considered above.

Such reconciliation as is possible depends upon how much of the force of 'self-imposed' can be borne by the 'agreement' to which a member is a party and, beyond that, upon the possible equivalence of 'participation' and 'self-imposition.'

Can the voluntary acceptance of membership be regarded as sufficient, by itself, to make the system of law and authority self-imposed? The difficulty is that even though membership is voluntary it also involves subordination; and it is hard to square the subordination, earlier described as to a decision 'other than one's own,' with self-imposition. This seems especially difficult in cases in which membership does not carry with it the right of further participation in the public decision-making process. Here membership, voluntary though it be, seems to entail the abdication of rule-making authority; we consent to being governed without our further consent; and even if withdrawal possibilities are preserved, I wonder if we would regard such abdication as adequately reconciling membership and freedom. Abdication is no less an abdication because it is voluntary. It does not look like 'self-government.'

Suppose, however, that we describe the acceptance of membership not in terms of abdication but rather as the 'delegation' of decision-making authority. 'Delegation' is a complex notion with two essential aspects. It involves both the assignment of a task and the entrusting with discretion. When the task or end is clearly defined and specific the element of discretion shrinks to the mere choice of means and the act of delegation has little of the quality of abdication; the agent seems to be our servant going about our business without threat to our freedom. But when the task is less clearly defined and requires significant 'interpretation' as well as implementation, the act of delegation takes on more of the quality of putting ourselves in other hands, and the hands of the servant begin to resemble the hands of a master. This is a difficult matter of degree and there has traditionally been great sensitivity at this point. Delegation becomes 'undue delegation' when it is inadequately directed and thus seems to come to the verge of abdication. To the extent that the acceptance of membership in a body politic can be described in terms of delegation it seems possible to reconcile membership with freedom, preserving a self-imposed character for the demands of law.

The difficulty, however, is that while much delegation satisfies the demand for adequate direction, some fundamental and crucial delegation of authority does not. The attempt to reconcile membership and freedom pushes on, therefore, to the assertion of a necessary relationship between membership and 'participation' which, since Rousseau at least, has made 'political freedom' and 'democracy' virtually synonymous. Membership, that is to say, does not satisfy the demand for freedom unless, in addition to its being voluntary, it involves participation in the exercise of sovereignty—so that each member, by virtue of this participation, is not only a subject but a 'maker' of the law.

Let me oversimplify. A number of individuals form a body politic, each agreeing to acknowledge the authority of the decision of the majority of the members. I pointed out earlier that this does involve the subordination of private decision. But at this stage the decision of the majority is arrived at by the participation of each member in the decision-making process. The question is whether such participation adequately preserves the self-imposed character of law. It is a step short of veto power, but it is as far as we can go in this direction. It is the solution of democracy—a body politic in which each (full) member is also a participant in the work of the highest decision-making tribunal.

The necessary subordination of private to public decision which inescapably confronts the member of a body politic with the obligation to acknowledge the authority of a decision with which he may disagree appears at best as 'delegation.' 'Participation' is not an alternative to 'delegation' but seems, rather, to protect it against degenerating into 'abdication.' How adequately the conception of voluntary membership in a group, in whose basic decisions the member participates, captures the sense of 'governing oneself' I must leave the reader to determine for himself. It goes a long way for me, considering that man is not a unanimous animal.

But there are additional difficulties. The sovereign majority cannot do very much itself. So it must delegate, to tribunals which themselves delegate. This is basic to the theory of representative government. But at every delegation the thread of participation grows thinner. Rousseau thought that a single delegation snapped it, and that Representative Government was slavery. Locke tolerated a delegation by the majority to Parliament before he declared that delegated powers cannot be redelegated. American problems in this area are too complex to describe in passing; they involve the seething world of administrative agencies, the oft-bemoaned tyranny of the 'government of men' instead of the 'rule of law,' etc.

So that even if we surmount the theoretical difficulty there is still the question of the adequacy and effectiveness of participation as the system of governing institutions proliferates, and discretion compounded by discretion presents the surprised, self-governing member with the results of 'his' decision. But the free citizen will refuse to abdicate. He will persist in the demand for constitutionality which, with all its complexity, reflects the vitality of the demand that government be the creature of agreement. Only by dint of ceaseless devotion to the task of keeping the delicate structure of consent, participation, and authority in good repair can we save the claim of self-government from being a bitter mockery.

Americans did not invent the social compact theory of the state. Nor is it, I would judge, held in very high esteem by contemporary political theorists. But fate has strangely tied us to it. We are the people of the Constitutional Convention, the great debate, the Union-creating ratification. Our constitution is not merely custom; it is a written charter of agreements and it begins with 'We, the People.' If, in the world today, we still represent an ideal toward which others move, it is the ideal of a body politic which has taken its destiny in its own hands and lives as a voluntary group whose citizens are parties to the social compact and participants in the governing process. Where we fall short, our failure is measured by the demands of this ideal; and elsewhere, wherever 'unauthorized' power still prevails, the call to arms is sounded in its terms. Every revolution won must accommodate itself to this conception of political life; every delay requires apology or excuse; every denial remorselessly sets the stage for the next act.

But more than this, the compact theory of the state is the great contribution of the Western secular mind to the hope for world peace. In a world of diverse creeds it provides the bedrock of universally intelligible moral and political conception upon which, if we escape disaster, the world community will erect its saving political institutions.

3

The Agent

AGENCY

The ruler who once thundered as the omnipotent father now comes disguised as Mr. Smith the errand-boy. A history of politics might well be written on that transformation. Man has long been a political animal, and his being ruled is as familiar as his unruliness. Experience has spawned a wide range of metaphor. We are a flock or a horde, a band of brothers or a collection of billiard balls, an harmonious organism or classes at war. But we can never forget the fact of government, and our awareness of the relation of ruler and ruled finds a variety of appropriate expressions. The tradition usually begins, naturally enough, with the conquest of chaos. The mess is cleared up, things are sorted out and put in their places, bedlam is rolled back, a garden is established in the wilderness. The lawgiver comes to power, fixes his canon, and we are off! History presents us in due time with the Shepherd, the Guardian, the Protector and Peacemaker, the Policeman, Rule-maker, Housekeeper, Broker, the Trustee, the Representative, the Public Servant, the Provider. Out of the mass of available notions I shall take as central the notion of the Agent. Thus I supplement 'being a member of' with 'being an agent of' a body politic and between the two exhaust the scope of political obligation.

Moving still within the framework of an 'agreement' theory of the state and assuming its inherent distinction between power and authority, I shall consider 'authorized agent' as generally redundant. The body politic is constituted by the authorization of an official decision-making institution whose voice the members acknowledge as binding. The decision, or the voice, is that of the agent, or agents. To be an agent is thus to be duly authorized to act in a special way.

I cannot refrain from calling attention, at this point, to the all too little known Chapter XVI of Part One of *Leviathan* in which Hobbes, moving beyond his earlier analyses, breaks new ground in abandoning 'contract' for the developing conceptions of 'agent' and 'representative.' The view that the sovereign is created by authorization is emphasized by the distinction Hobbes makes between a 'natural' and an 'artificial' person. A natural person is one whose actions are merely his own; an artificial person is one whose acts are to be taken as the acts of another. The sovereign, as an artificial person, is thus one who is authorized to represent or to act for others.

The political agent is one who is authorized to act on behalf of, or in the name of, others—the members, or the body politic. Let me point out some of the obvious features of this relationship. First, the actions of the agent, in the name of the body politic, are binding upon the members and create obligations for them. Second, acting for the body politic, the agent is responsible for a range of interests, goods, or purposes distinguishable from his own, as, so to speak, a natural or private person. Thus, the distinction between public and private forces its way into the very conception of the public agent. He is one who is given responsibility for the achievement or pursuit of public purpose. Third, there are some difficulties in the way of giving a too simple answer to the question '*whose* agent?'. He may be chosen or designated by a part of the body politic, his own constituency; but he is chosen to take his place in a tribunal which is itself the agent of the whole. We are familiar with the pressures which lead the agent to see himself primarily as the agent of his constituency and which thus tend to transform tribunal colleagues into a collection of ambassadors. But in the face of this tendency we need to consider less how the agent got there than what he is when he gets there. He may be the Senator *from* a particular state but he is, after all, a Senator of the United States, manning a tribunal of the whole body politic. Moreover, 'body politic' in this context has a time-spanning feature which brings into consideration as members our as yet unborn children. If it seems metaphysical nonsense to speak of 'non-existent members,' for whom are we planning the kindergartens of 1970? The country does not belong entirely to the living. The 'public' and the 'body politic' are far from simple notions, and the theory of agency dares not be hasty or crude at this point.

To be an agent is thus to accept authority or assume responsibility. And this acceptance involves a subordination which calls to mind the subordination entailed by the acceptance of membership. It involves, for the agent, the subordination of private interest to public interest. And it demands, although perhaps in a different way, the disciplining of judgment. His role requires that he pursue certain goals in certain ways, which may not be entirely *his* goals or *his* ways. There are other points of comparison. Just as the member finds his status protected by certain fundamental

'rights,' so also the agent claims certain basic 'powers' necessary for the adequate discharge of his duty—a fact which
has special significance for the understanding of the complex problems of civil rights and civil liberties in a democratic polity. And, not least, the loyalty of the member has
its counterpart in the loyalty of the agent to his role or
function.

The attempt to find a concept which adequately captures
the significant features of the agreement-based relation of
ruler to ruled has often ended in the choice of a 'legal' concept. 'Contract' is, perhaps, most familiar. But I share with
Hobbes the conviction that 'agency' is, all in all, more appropriate and that it is especially useful for the analysis of
'representative' government.

'To represent' has several different senses. In one sense it
means to 'stand for' or to symbolize, as a flag represents or
as a figurehead or monarch who reigns but does not rule
represents; it is ceremonial representation. But in another
sense 'to represent' is not 'to stand for' but 'to act for.'
Here the representative and the agent seem to come together and characteristic ambiguities appear in both. Does
'acting for' mean simply carrying out orders or does it
mean acting in the interests of the represented? There is
quite a difference, and there are different conceptions of
representative government stemming from this difference.
Sometimes we expect the representative to act as our in-
structed delegate. But sometimes we expect him to do his
Burkean best, in spite of our harassment. We are not too
clear, unanimous, or consistent at this point.

Ambiguity appears also when we think of the representative body, a parliament or a legislature. On the one hand
its representativeness is thought to be that of a 'sample'; a
legislature is representative when it contains within itself

the same elements, in the same proportion, as are found in the body politic at large. It is typical of us; we are all in it in microcosm. As such, it mirrors or reflects; what we think, it thinks; what it does, we do; it is simply the body politic writ small. Behind this conception are marshaled the attempts to make our representative institutions more representative. They should be like us so they will act like us—no better, no worse.

On the other hand there still lingers the conception of representative government as a form of elective aristocracy. And on this view we want to be represented by our best, our wisest and fairest. The representative body should be the cream, not a homogenized sample. It should not mirror, but focus; its sense should be uncommon; its vision clearer. But it is still our agent, acting for the body politic. We move restlessly between these two conceptions of representative government, indignant when our desires are ignored, indignant when they are indulged. We reject the Statesman for the Politician and then scorn the Politician for not being a Statesman. While this is too complicated an issue to settle out of hand, I risk the judgment that the conception of the representative body as a representative sample is a futile and fatal one. The representative, the public agent, had better be us at our best, not at our most typical.

I suggested earlier that a theory of political obligation was concerned with providing the elements of such answers as are possible to the agent's 'what should I do?'. The public agent is one who is authorized to act in the name of and on behalf of the body politic; he has a task related to some aspect of the public good and he has a measure of discretion. I do not think there is very much more that can profitably be said at this level of abstraction. It is necessary now to place the agent into the context in which he does his work and in which he appears not simply as a political agent but as a legislator, or administrator, or judge, or elector, activating or manning a particular decision-making institution, itself only a part of the system of institutions which, taken together, we call the Government.

The Tribunal Context

It will be convenient to refer to any decision-making or policy-making institution as a 'tribunal.' I use the term indiscriminately to cover a range of institutions which differ from each other in many ways. A court is a tribunal, as is a legislature, or an administrative agency or board. So is an electorate or an institution as complex as the 'amending power.' I do not intend, in using the term widely, to suggest that all decision-making institutions are really 'courts,' or to suggest that governing is the episodic production of discrete acts of decision. It is simply that the agent is not on his own but takes his place as a member of some decision-making institution. He mans a tribunal.

A tribunal is itself a part of a system of tribunals and much of its special character depends upon the character of the system and its place within it, so that it can hardly be understood except in its systemic context. The study of the system of tribunals from a variety of points of view is, of course, a traditional concern of political science.

A system is not simply a 'heap' of tribunals. It embodies an organized structure of authority, a network of delegation, a division of functions or tasks. The structure of the system seems, inescapably, to be hierarchical. This suggests that a pervasive feature of government is a strong sense of echelon, an awareness of up and down, of subordination and superordination. A tribunal will normally have both a supervisory or overruling function and a deferential or contributory function, both of which deeply affect its dealing with a problem; its vertical preoccupation may, in fact, become so great as to leave little room for anything else—a disease which might be called the 'escalator effect.' But even at best, tribunals seldom confront external problems *de novo*, uncomplicated by a history of previous treatment and the promise of subsequent review.

Hierarchy suggests, in addition to a vertical dimension, the converging of parallel structures, or perhaps branches, at an apex. Somewhere, the monster has a head. This means that in any system of tribunals there is a highest tribunal from whose judgment or decision there is no appeal to another tribunal. This has generally been called the sovereign tribunal and its jurisdiction marks the limits of the body politic. The theory of sovereignty has different aspects, but one of them is simply the affirmation of the hierarchical character of government culminating in a single most authoritative tribunal, which is not only the highest court of appeal but also the source of such authority as is delegated to the subordinate tribunals within the system.

Concepts of hierarchy and sovereignty tend to arouse concern over the concentration, centralization, or monopoly of power; so that while we recognize, especially when it is lacking, the need for co-ordination and unity, we also look to the dispersion, delegation, or diffusion of authority as providing an inherent defense against undue or dangerous concentration. We are thus led to supplement hierarchy with demands for 'checks and balances' and for the 'separation of powers.'

The demand for the separation of powers seems based on the view that there are distinct classes of tasks or functions and that a particular tribunal should be limited to a single class of tasks. Thus we distinguish traditionally the legislative, administrative or executive, and judicial functions, and when we insist on the separation of powers we insist that these functions be performed by distinct tribunals, presumably even independent of each other. We are not too clear about the difference between these functions and, in any case, there is considerable mythology in vogue at this point.

We think of the legislative tribunal as the law-making body and sometimes are disturbed by the discovery that administrative tribunals make rules or that courts in interpreting laws seem to be rewriting them. Or we discover that the executive does more than meekly carry out the law and bemoan this as an invasion of the legislature's sphere, little realizing that the poor executive is trying to recapture some of the policy prerogative wrested from him earlier by an encroaching legislature. There is probably some point to distinguishing between law making, executing, and adjudicating, but the use of 'legislative,' 'executive' and 'judicial' as names for branches of government should not mislead us into oversimplified views of altogether distinct and exclusive functions.

There are, however, several significant demands of which we must take account. We want a person accused of a crime to be tried before a court with traditions and procedures designed to determine individual guilt or innocence fairly and dispassionately. We object to legislative bodies moving into this field in the guise of passing laws which are bills of attainder, essentially legislative declarations of individual guilt, or in the guise of investigation. We are concerned when administrative agencies set up tribunals to judge individuals on the basis of procedures inappropriate to a court; or when a legislature uses its power of appropriation to control specific administrative appointments. Issues of this sort raise jurisdictional questions not so much out of concern for the purity of rather crude classifications of functions, but out of the concern that particular tasks be performed by the tribunals which are best equipped to handle them and which have been given primary responsibility. 'Separation of powers!' in this context is a call for proper jurisdiction.

'Check and balance!' is a battle-cry with a different point. It means that we want policy, as it is promulgated, executed, and enforced, to be shaped by the impact of a variety of tribunals dominated by different traditions and viewpoints. What emerges from the folk-like legislature as popularly tolerable policy gets tossed into the hands of the experienced, professional administrator for reshaping in the process of implementation. But these bureaucrats who have neither met a payroll nor won an election are tackled by a horde of sharp black-letter lawyers defending this or that client or interest, and end up arguing before an independent and often unsympathetic bench about what they can or cannot do. Policy must run this gauntlet beyond the protection of its friends, and this ordeal is assured by the fact that the tribunal that approves or launches policy does not carry it out, interpret, or judge it. If this is the point of checks and balances, as I think it is, we can well understand our alternate feelings of exasperation over botched results and of reassurance at the spectacle of hierarchical power held in check.

Part of the problem of understanding any tribunal is to see its special character as shaped by its relations with other tribunals in the system. The system is the broader context, as the particular tribunal is the immediate context, within which the agent works. Abstracted from this context an abstract question gets an abstract answer. To 'what should I do?' in general, the unilluminating reply is 'do the right thing'; just as to 'what should I believe?' we answer, 'the truth.' Seeking a level of abstraction at which the answer to 'what should I do?' is relevant to *any* agent, although not especially helpful to any particular agent, we offer up 'pursue the appropriate purpose with proper procedure and with respect for relevant law.'

This formula suggests, to no one's surprise, that the elements of proper conduct for the agent are purpose, law, and procedure. What purpose? What law? What procedure? Here again we must turn for concrete guidance to the tribunal context and draw from the character of the particular tribunal such answers as it provides.

Public Purpose

I begin, rather nervously, with the assertion that any art or artifact supports a teleological question and that it is appropriate to ask about the purpose of a tribunal or a system of tribunals. We are, perhaps, more comfortable with 'function' than with 'purpose,' but function, while it has a broader range, is, when applied to artifacts, at least crypto-purposive. Thus, 'how does the heart function?' may be answerable without purposive overtones, but if we ask 'what is the function of a carburetor?' no theological issue is raised if the answer is 'the purpose of the carburetor is to . . .' So, questions about the function of the Cabinet or the Joint-Chiefs or the Rules Committee are, in part, answerable by 'it is supposed to . . .' or 'its job or purpose is . . .' We judge tribunals as ill-designed or well-designed and this assumes a task to be performed. A public tribunal, in short, has a purpose or purposes; it is the guardian of some end or good or value, however well- or ill-defined or even half-forgotten.

The tribunal purpose is a *public* purpose, and that qualification reminds us that there are many human purposes for which government or public authority makes no provision. We are always asking whether government should not undertake something more, or perhaps asserting that it is undertaking too much, and this suggests that we do not exhaust the meaning of 'public purpose' in identifying it with the range of purposes assigned to the system of tribunals at any particular time. That is to say, the class of 'legitimate public purposes' may not be identical with the class of 'undertaken public purposes'; there may be legitimate purposes or tasks not assigned to any tribunal within a system, and it is possible that some assigned tasks may not be proper ones for government to undertake.

'Legitimate' itself, as applied to public purpose, has several meanings. In one sense it means simply assigned or authorized. Thus, for example, a tribunal authorized to control floods in an area may undertake also to develop and provide public power; and the question may be raised as to whether that is a legitimate, i.e. authorized, purpose for it to undertake. A negative answer would not settle the question of whether the development of public power might be a legitimate public purpose, i.e. an appropriate or proper task for government. The distinction can be expressed simply as the difference between 'legitimate for this tribunal' and 'legitimate for government.' The former involves the relatively simple question of whether in fact a tribunal has been delegated the authority to deal with a problem; the latter raises more difficult questions about the proper aims or scope of government.

To assert a distinction between 'legitimate' and 'undertaken' public purpose is to deny that the authority of the sovereign tribunal is unlimited. Such a denial, as I suggested earlier, is implicit in any agreement theory of the state. But the difficulties involved in clarifying the limits of sovereign authority are great. Suppose, for example, that a constitutional amendment is adopted in the United States, by due action of the amending-power, giving Congress authority to enact legislation for the purpose of ensuring the eternal salvation of American citizens. Would we say that the sovereign has spoken and that this is now a legitimate purpose of our government? If not, how would we argue that the sovereign has exceeded its authority and pursues an illegitimate public purpose?

Keeping in mind the troublesome but inescapable distinction between the given or undertaken and the legitimate, it is still the case that the system of tribunals, in one of its aspects, embodies a system of public purposes. The agent, taking his place within a tribunal, finds himself involved in its purpose and gets from that purpose a part of the answer to his 'what should I do?'.

Law

While from one point of view the tribunal system is seen as the reflection of a structure of public purpose it can also be regarded as the creator and sustainer of a structure of laws, rules, norms, or even principles—evolving and developing a system of constitutional principles, legislation, ordinances, rulings, standards. The state, if we squint in this way, is seen as a 'legal order'; government, a rule of law—its every act required by, or in conformity with, a pre-existing rule or law.

There *is* a web of law generally co-extensive with the system of tribunals, and we think of it as sharing the hierarchical character of the system. We work away at keeping it consistent, in the sense that legislation is supposed to be in conformity with constitutional principles, administrative rules in conformity with legislation. If at times we alter the higher to accommodate the lower we generally expect the lower to defer to the demands of what is higher in the hierarchy of law.

A particular tribunal is, therefore, not only possessed of a purpose but is involved in a system of law, and the action of its agents must accommodate itself to this fact. 'Hierarchy' reminds us, at this point, that for any tribunal within the system some laws or rules are given, emanate from a higher authority, and can be changed only by a higher tribunal. Whatever interpretive scope there may be, Congress did not create and cannot alter the provisions of the constitution, just as the I.C.C. did not enact and cannot repeal the congressional legislation with which its rulings must be consistent.

But a tribunal not only finds itself subject to higher laws which it must take as given; it is itself a creator of law and often finds itself increasingly confined by a web of its own spinning. Each of its actions tends, willy-nilly, to become a precedent, a budding rule; the intra-office memo soon becomes a part of the public domain; and the demand for consistent, predictable action is felt even before the tribunal promulgates, in the form appropriate for it, 'law.'

Nor is this all. Inferior or subordinate tribunals, exercising their discretion, shape a hint into a body of rules which the delegating tribunal generally finds itself helpless to do much but recognize. It can, in principle, overrule, but it is seldom in a position to meddle, and even with the worst of intentions it is not omnipresent.

The tribunal context thus provides the agent not only with purposive direction but with principles, laws, or rules of which he is the guardian. To some degree he is a rule-maker, shaping rules to demands of the tribunal purpose; to some degree we see him as the defender of a legal order.

Procedure

Procedure, as we consider the tribunal system, takes us beyond the state of dreamy, purposive aspiration or torpid, rule-bound stirring, and strikes our much-loved dynamic note. Tribunals *do* things, agents act. But how they act is a matter of great importance, not only in terms of results, for the sake of which much is forgiven, but in terms of the propriety of method. The appropriateness of procedure, as it has evolved from trial by combat and omen-reading, turns on two factors. First, there is an 'objective' side, a problem to solve, a difficulty to surmount. Method or procedure is judged adequate or inadequate as it meets this objective aspect of the situation. Second, in the face of disagreement and conflicts of interest and purpose, we demand that procedure be fair or, in another sense of the term, 'objective' or disinterested. We ask that procedure be 'reasonable' in both senses of that term: adequately result-producing, and fair. There are temptations in both directions. Preoccupation with results may lead to impatience in suffering 'fools' or 'obvious scoundrels.' On the other hand, we are sometimes so concerned over our disagreements that we are led, out of a misconception about fairness, to want to satisfy all parties, to give something to everyone, in short, to compromise. This is our great procedural golden calf, whose worship will destroy us. It is, as I suggested, a misconception about fairness; but its great defect is that it simply does not produce decisions which are adequate to meet the problem, however happy it keeps us temporarily. But this is a theme I hope to develop elsewhere.

The other general aspect of the procedural problem I wish to mention is the span covered by 'mere process' through 'due process' to 'substantive due process.' There is a minimal way of going through the motions which hardly satisfies us—the hearing at which no one listens. More than this is 'due.' But even due process sometimes produces odd results, and we tend in our stricter moods to exclude certain results as the miscarriage of procedure, no matter how diligent or careful.

Procedure, like purpose and law, is built into the tribunal context. Every tribunal has its way of doing things, partly a reflection of the character of its task, partly a reflection of the general procedural demands of the system. There may be some tension between the general demands and the particular necessities, and tribunals overwhelmed by the latter may often be impatient with the procedural demands of the system. But the agent, here too, is not on his own. He joins a going concern and needs, at least, to learn its ways before he is taken seriously as a procedure-mender.

This brief consideration of public purpose, law, and procedure, as they are embodied in a system of tribunals, leaves more questions unanswered than problems solved. But they are the significant features of any tribunal system and the keys to any theory of the obligation of the public agent.

Purpose, law, and procedure have each been taken as basic and made the cornerstone of a theory of the state. Thus we have the 'Purposive State,' the community organized to achieve its goals, acting through its purposive agents. From this point of view the law and procedure are instrumental, adaptable to and subordinate to public ends. I shall not parade the virtues of this view, but point instead to the fears it evokes. First, there is some fear that public purpose is a hungry category, devouring and absorbing the private; it has, it is said, a totalitarian appetite. And second, whenever 'ends' are stressed we half expect to hear that the end justifies the means and that red tape, archaic law, or the niceties of procedure will not stand in the way of holy purpose. The purposive theory of the state needs to face these fears and provide some assurance.

Taking law as central we develop theories of the state as a legal order or as the 'rule of law.' The state is a group of men living within a hierarchical framework of law to which, in the pursuit of their private purposes, they conform. The structure of law may need occasional mending, and it needs to be supported with sanctions; but beyond this, public purpose, except for defense, which is really an extension of law and order, is an unwarranted intrusion. *The* public purpose is to provide the legal framework within which private purpose plays. This is a theory of a limited, unobtrusive state congenial to those who like to think of enterprise as private. But it has given ground in the face of necessary public enterprise. It offers to the community trying to shape its own destiny in a changing world only the solace of the policeman, the lawyer, and the court.

Procedure, too, has its devotees. Substance, we are told, is secreted in the interstices of procedure. Purpose is raw ✓ material, law a temporary crystallization; but the life of government is its process. Democrats seem especially inclined to emphasize this aspect of government, to stress the commitment to 'the democratic process,' to 'majority rule,' or, perhaps, to the 'process of compromise.' And we hear much more frequently that the democratic citizen is expected to participate in the political process than that he is expected to be a guardian of public purpose. Procedure is important, and certain features of procedure may well provide a significant basis for the classification of states; but procedure is not an end in itself and needs always to be judged purposively.

But whether the stress is on purpose, law, or procedure it cannot be denied that all are involved and interrelated and that a theory of political obligation must come to terms with all three.

I have argued that the agent finds in the tribunal context significant clues to conduct. I seem, in fact, to be saying that once the agent finds his place in a tribunal the rest is given. There is the tribunal purpose, the framework of law, the standard procedure. What else is needed to answer his questions about his duties and obligations?

Does this not seem too easy? The question, 'What ought I to do?' comes, in our age, clothed in mystery and anguish. In quest of answers we search for bits of significance in an absurd tumult. At least, we say, the 'ought' is not the 'is,' the ideal is not the given, the normative not the descriptive. How then can it be said, so casually, that the public agent's 'ought' finds its answer in what is 'given' by the nature of the tribunal? Let me try a short answer where a long one is called for.

There is a poignant ambiguity in 'what should I do?'. It is one thing when asked by an individual seeking to fill a role; it is another when asked by one seeking a role to fill. In the latter form it is really 'what should I be?'. And we know the terrible force of this question in what we call an individualistic, dynamic, open society. 'You can choose,' we are told, 'find or make your own place, pick the part that suits you.' And so we search, individuals in search of a character in search of an author. 'Is there a script, is there a part for me, for what am I cast, what am I good for?' 'What,' in short, 'should I do with myself?' I do not know how to answer this question except in terms of the traditional wisdom: find a task, a part to play, a role which uses and develops your talents in a significant human enterprise; or else, in despair of a significant enterprise, cultivate your garden and die.

But civilization, even in disarray, has its significant enterprises and presents us with a variety of roles. And a role is a complex of duties and obligations, of lore and discipline, of purpose, principle, and procedure. When, as apprenticed to a role, we ask 'what should I do?' we ask no longer the questing 'what should I be?' but rather 'what is required of me?' here and now, in this place and this time. What are the duties of this station? Thus, for the political agent, the tribunal defines his role.

But while much is given, what is given is not enough to reduce an art to a routine. There are complexities which constantly pose problems of decision. But beyond that there remains an inescapable tension between the given and the appropriate or the ideal which leaves the agent rooted in the one and plagued by the other. This *is* the procedure; but it is not as good as it should be. This *is* the law; but it is not quite just. This *is* our purpose; but it is only an incomplete fragment. The agent must take what is given, follow and enforce; but he must also improve. The role is played in different styles. At one extreme the agent is the child of the established fact, doing 'what is done,' timidly precedent-minded, discretion-shunning, fort-holding. Others, in varying degree and with varying insight and capacity, are restless with mere habit, innovating, and creative. They are no less agents for being also the agents of our groping, inarticulate aspirations. But here the agent becomes what the states-

V man always is—the teacher who helps us to clarify and understand our purposes, perfect our law, and make our procedures more rational.

The Transformation of Conflict

There may have been an age of contentment, but ours surely is one of contention. We need no reminder of the pervasiveness of conflict, competition, opposition. Like Heraclitus musing over the bow and the lyre, we see harmony as the result of pulling in opposite directions. Thesis and antithesis produce a higher synthesis; competition, a higher order of achievement; the struggle for existence, the evolutionary process—these are still lingering dogmas. But we are less sanguine now about the invisible hand, less inclined to let conflict run an unchecked course. We seek, in various ways, to guide human conflict, to tame or transform it, to civilize.

Recent ethical theory has made much of the distinction between two kinds of opposition or disagreement: between disagreement in belief, or cognitive disagreement, and disagreement in attitude, or non-cognitive disagreement. Cognitive disagreement occurs when two propositions are asserted, both of which cannot be true; that is, when the truth of one proposition is incompatible with the truth of the other. Non-cognitive disagreement is more difficult to explain. Let me say, roughly, that it involves 'opposing' desires, the satisfaction of which are incompatible. I stress the fact of incompatibility, although this may narrow the notion a bit. For example, 'some politicians are dishonest' and 'some politicians are honest' is not a case of cognitive disagreement since both propositions might be true and no conflict involved. Similarly, 'I like politicians' and 'I don't like politicians' might, as statements, both be true and, in that case, report different attitudes toward politicians. This difference might be called by some a disagreement in attitude; but I shall here reserve this notion for cases like 'I want to win' versus 'I want to win'—both true as statements but incompatible in the sense that the satisfaction of one expressed desire precludes the satisfaction of the other. It should be pointed out that settling a cognitive disagreement involves showing, or trying to show, that one of the statements is true. This is not the case with non-cognitive disagreement since desires or attitudes are neither true nor false and since the statements which express or report incompatible desires can both be true. Thus, the cognitive disagreement between 'all politicians are dishonest' and 'some politicians are not dishonest' is settled by the finding of some honest politicians. But the conflict between 'we want you to pay us higher wages' and 'we don't want to pay you higher wages' is not settled by showing that one or both statements are indeed true.

Awareness of this distinction helps us to avoid the error of supposing that all conflicts or disagreements can be settled simply by looking for the truth. But while the distinction between cognitive and non-cognitive disagreement seems obvious, I wish to point to a common feature relevant to the problems of dealing with conflict.

Allowing myself some terminological latitude, I wish to suggest a distinction between the 'assertive' and the 'claiming' mood—a distinction which cuts across the one between cognitive and non-cognitive. Consider statements like 'in my opinion all politicians are dishonest' or 'I believe all politicians are dishonest'; also, 'I want more money.' Let me call such expressions assertive; they express or assert a state of belief or desire. It is apparent that, unlike the earlier example, 'I believe all politicians are dishonest' and 'I believe some politicians are not dishonest' are *not* in cognitive disagreement. Baffled in the attempt to establish the claim to truth of 'all politicians are dishonest,' we retreat to 'well, I believe . . .' Whether we reserve, waive, or abandon the claim, some retreat is involved; we merely assert. Similarly, 'I want more money' expresses or asserts a state of desire. It makes no claims.

In contrast, 'all politicians are dishonest' or 'it is true that all politicians are dishonest' are in the claiming mood. The fact of belief does not settle the claim; something more is claimed than that I believe something. The parallel claiming mood for 'I want more money' would be 'I am entitled to more money.'

What I am suggesting, in short, in this parallel:

'I believe P' is related to 'P is true'

as

'I want X' is related to 'I am entitled to X.'

The second in each pair makes a claim beyond what is simply asserted by the first.

The point of this digression is that the civilizing of conflict involves the movement from the assertive to the claiming mood. In the face of mere assertiveness, whether of belief or of desire, what is there to do but stand baffled, draw lines, and unleash the dogs of war? But in the face of claim and counter-claim we can go to work. As, in fact, we have long been at work. A good part of the history of civilization is the story of the creation of disciplines, techniques, and institutions of ordeal by which beliefs are tested, validated, warranted, confirmed, proved. It is one thing to assert belief; it is quite another thing to have a 'right' to a belief. We establish a right to a belief when we confirm its claim to 'truth.' Whatever their shortcomings there are methods and tests, the institutions of the scientific or cognitive enterprise. They are so well established that we often forget the achievement they represent in marking the road from assertion to claim to validation.

But what of the path from 'I want X,' through claim, to title? Here, too, we have been at work creating and developing the institutions for adjudicating and confirming conflicting claims, imposing 'rightness' upon 'wanting' as we have imposed 'truth' upon 'believing.' The laboratory and the court are companion institutions for the confirming of claims.

While this is, I think, a useful parallel, it raises many questions which I cannot pursue. I linger for a single comment. Confirming claims seems to involve two notions: a *process* of probing, testing, examining; and some conception of an 'objective' order or standard to which some sort of 'correspondence' is demanded. Belief and desire are sometimes thought of as 'subjective' and in need of correction if they do not match up with 'objective reality.' It is at this point that the challenge to the parallel is usually made. Science, it is said, is one thing; there is a process of testing beliefs, *and* there is a 'real,' objective order to which our beliefs, when true, conform. But justice, for example, is an abstraction, or 'relative,' so that while there may be a process of ordeal and trial, the element of correspondence with an 'objective reality' is lacking. And this is fatal to the attempt at drawing a parallel between science and ethics. If this objection can be met, it would seem to be in one of two directions. One can attempt some defense of a conception of an objective justice or 'good'—a long and bumpy road. Or one can sit back quietly and observe the interesting spectacle of current philosophies of science rejecting, in the name of operationalism or conventionalism or even pragmatism, the notion of 'correspondence' or of 'objective reality' as relevant or appropriate to the cognitive enterprise.

I come now to the role of the tribunal or system of tribunals in transforming the character and course of conflict. In short order, it is this: the existence of a tribunal with jurisdiction over an area of conflict compels assertiveness to give way to claiming and provides the procedures, principles and purposes by which the claims are tested, disallowed, or confirmed. Thus, 'we want segregated schools' and 'we want integrated schools' brought into the tribunal must transform themselves (disguise themselves, perhaps, but even that is significant) into 'segregation is constitutional' and 'segregation is unconstitutional'—'constitutional' here being the form taken by 'just' or 'proper' or 'right.' This is what is demanded by the tribunal, for which the bare assertion of desires is only a fact in a complex situation, the genesis of a problem, not the terms of its solution. Where the tribunal decision governs the situation, argument must take a form relevant to its demands. I can no longer say 'I want this.' I must say to the tribunal, 'Your purposes, rules, and procedures require that you do this.' I must address myself to the agent's 'what should I do?' and show, if I can, that *his* duty requires that he do so and so. Thus I become, reluctantly perhaps, a claimant, reshaping my assertiveness to the demands of the tribunal context, pledged, if I have 'put myself on the country,' to accept the verdict, subject to sanctions if I do not.

The significance of this transforming function of the tribunal is difficult to exaggerate. It is comparable, in its effect upon social life, to the effect of the acceptance of the

authority of 'scientific method' upon our intellectual life.
It supplants the primitive duel and the primitive but still
persistent 'rite of bargain' as modes of conflict resolution.
These die hard, and in the area of international relations
still hold a large part of the field. Here our conflicts are
still in search of a tribunal, and we wander toward summits,
pausing on slopes, arguing in powerless assemblies or in
veto-bound councils. Bargaining is, no doubt, better than
fighting; but woe unto those who have no seat at the table. *Phrases*

The importance of the tribunal in conflict situations
should not lead us to suppose that tribunals are only peace-
making. Other common needs and goals, other problems,
lie behind the creation of many tribunals whose existence
testifies to our purposive as well as our combative bent. Co-
operation needs its institutions also. Peace may be an indispensable condition, but culture has goals beyond that,
for which we create tribunals to marshal intelligence for
fruitful action.

PUBLIC QUESTIONS

With what sort of questions or issues is the public agent
concerned? Or, to put it another way, what is a public question or issue? The suggestion I advance here is that a public question is a question which is properly raised before
or within a public tribunal. Does this exclude anything?
Or too little, or too much?

First, let us consider whether certain questions may be
excluded on the ground that since it is the job of a tribunal to *do* something only practical rather than speculative or theoretical questions are properly admissible. There
is, no doubt, considerable interest in the question of

whether or not there is a God, but would we consider this a question which falls within the jurisdiction of a public tribunal? It apparently is a public question as to whether religious schools should be tax-exempt, whether office-holders should be subject to religious tests, or whether a particular religion should be 'established.' These all require some sort of action; and such action may be based on convictions about the truth of certain religious doctrines. But there seems to be a difference here which would support the view that a public tribunal has no business or authority to rule on the speculative question, although it has authority to rule on some practical matters which are closely related to it. Nevertheless, we are familiar with states in which such questions of 'doctrine' do fall within the authority of a public tribunal. And this raises the question of whether the attempt to confine public questions to non-speculative, 'action' questions is a characteristic or peculiarity of tribunal systems only within a particular tradition. I confess that I would like to defend the view that the practical, active character of public tribunals would support the exclusion of theoretical questions from the class of public questions—i.e. questions properly before a public tribunal. But this rests on some complex views about the relation of theory and practice, mind and body, knowing and doing, and even sacred and secular or spiritual and material: views which have found expression, in our tradition, in theories of the separation of church and state or of the private and public domains. The complexity of these issues leads me to forgo the attempt to defend here the insistence on the limitation of public questions to action questions. But there remains, in any case, an interesting and significant difference between a tribunal's judgment that 'this is true' and its decision that 'this is to be done.' Posing the agent's

question as 'what should I do?' lends some support to the
appropriateness and relevance of the distinction between
practical and theoretical or speculative questions.

A public question is a question with which a public tri- ✓
bunal is authorized to deal; it falls within its jurisdiction.
With respect to any subordinate tribunal within a system
the problem of whether a question is properly before it
presents only minor difficulties. Thus, 'did Smith commit
this crime?' is a question not properly before a legislature,
but it is a public question, properly before a public tribunal—a court. There are borderline jurisdictional questions between tribunals, but I pass them by, since usually
the question is which public tribunal is appropriate. The
interesting issue arises when we consider whether certain
questions are beyond the jurisdiction of the whole system
of public tribunals or beyond the jurisdiction of even the
highest tribunal within the system.

Put in simple form, and in the American context, the
issue is: Are there some questions which cannot properly be
placed before the amending power? If not, why not? Consider the constitutional amendment which provides that
Congress shall make no law respecting an establishment of
religion. This means that the question of establishing a
religion is not properly before Congress as a public tribunal,
not a public question for *it*. But is it not a question appropriately, however foolishly, raised before the amending
power in the form of a proposed amendment? Is it not
within its jurisdiction?

The denial of this possibility sometimes takes the form
of asserting that the constitutional guarantee in question is
itself gratuitous, that it is merely declarative of inherent
limits upon public authority and not really a self-denying
ordinance. This position is taken, I think, to avoid the nat-

ural inference that if the promulgating or amending power has authority to promulgate a rule it can also modify or abolish the rule. To regard the Bill of Rights as merely 'declarative' is to rest upon a higher law doctrine which puts limits to the jurisdiction of even the highest tribunal within the system. Certain questions, on this view, are not public questions.

Beyond the assertion that there are limits to the jurisdiction of public tribunals, the nature of those limits is seldom made very clear. Is what I drink a private matter beyond consideration by public authority? Is who or how often or how many I marry a private question? Or is who, or with what rites, I worship a private matter or a matter for a church to decide? Is who or how to hire and fire a private matter for a corporation to decide? There is no doubt that within our system many decisions or questions are declared to be beyond the jurisdiction of the subordinate public tribunals. That this is so is a fact which we sometimes describe as 'pluralism.' That this must or should be so is also supposedly dictated by 'pluralism,' but I confess I have never found the theory to be more than a reiteration of the arrangement. Of course there are private decisions. Of course there are economic and social and religious institutions making decisions in which public authority does not intervene. But *should* it intervene is itself a public question properly posed, if nowhere else, before the amending power. There we may argue wisdom or folly, but to do so is to concede jurisdiction. There, perhaps, we may also argue jurisdiction, reminding the sovereign of the limits to the grant of authority implicit in the basic authorization. And here we encounter again, with no better results, our old friend 'who is to judge?'.

'Politicality' or 'publicness' is not a simple property or

quality which some questions do have and some do not. Our distinctions between public and private reflect our arrangements rather than guide or dictate them. For all the subordinate tribunals within a system the question of the ultimate jurisdiction of public authority does not arise. Each has its admittedly limited jurisdiction over a limited class of questions properly raised before it. Only for the 'sovereign' tribunal does the ultimate question arise. I do not know how reassuring it is to realize that this tribunal is also the most popular and least expert one in the system. It is also the most difficult to mobilize or activate.

The way in which an issue or question is raised in or presented to a tribunal varies considerably and depends upon the place or function of the tribunal within a system as well as upon its own rules. But whether raised by appeal to it, or on the initiative of a member of the tribunal, or by mandate from above, public issues have a common form: 'the tribunal ought to do X.' Variably in this form we have, for example: 'the court ought to issue this writ,' or 'the F.C.C. ought to grant this permit,' or 'the agency ought to approve this project,' or 'the council ought to pass this ordinance.' Whatever argument, evidence, or deliberation develops is brought to a focus in this form whether, from the outside the demand is 'you should do this' or from the inside the question is 'should we do this?' or 'what should we do about this?'. The procedures and style of deliberation vary, but about this central form.

To say that the question is within the jurisdiction of the tribunal is to say that it involves an appeal to, or the implementation of, the purposes and/or the laws which, as I discussed earlier, define the function of that tribunal. I do not wish to suggest a sharp separation of purpose and law or that they are not intimately related, but, for what I think are sufficient reasons, I suggest we consider separately the different problems presented by the dominance in a particular situation of the factor of purpose or of the factor of law. Thus, I now distinguish, within the common form, two varieties of public issues: (1) Doing X is required by or will satisfy the *purpose* of the tribunal, and (2) doing X is required by or will satisfy the *law* of which the tribunal is guardian.

The difference between the appeal to purpose and the appeal to law is the difference between the two great moods of deliberative life, which I shall call respectively the purposive or pragmatic mood and the casuistic mood. In the pragmatic mood we are goal-directed, aiming, selecting or creating means, predicting, and calculating. In the casuistic mood we are norm-centered, adjusting to the demand of rule or law, squaring ourselves with principle, legitimacy-minded. The interplay of purpose and law, I repeat, is constant; but the difference in emphasis justifies separate, if only temporarily separate, analysis. We are not sufficiently aware of this point of difference in our public questions or sufficiently attentive to the different problems posed by public questions like 'is segregation compatible with the fourteenth amendment?' and questions like 'how can we stop inflation?'.

The Pragmatic Mood

The pragmatic mood, using this term loosely, is the mood in which we are dominantly concerned with the achievement of purpose, with the means-end relationship. This is more complicated than may appear, and I begin with a caricature of the 'naïve' view which, I suppose, no one holds. According to this view some dominant parental tribunal, typically a legislature, promulgates laws, and turns them over to the courts and the police to enforce; decides on goals, ends, or purposes, which are turned over to other tribunals or administrators to reach or achieve. The process by which this is done is called 'politics,' and this covers a multitude of sins, including the sin of eating the forbidden fruit of the knowledge of good and evil. For this sin the politician is, of course, sooner or later thrust out of Eden, but in the meantime he presumes to take upon himself the burden of making 'value judgments.' But the other tribunals, thus relieved of this burden, need only make 'factual judgments.' They can be happy, guiltless, technicians achieving the given purpose unless, tempted by the Serpent, or Oedipus-like if you prefer, they yearn for the forbidden fruit and sneakily steal a policy bite. But this is to trespass, to forget the proper function, to violate the separation of powers. Acting properly, the 'administrative' tribunal dutifully applies itself to achieving the purpose given it. The 'what should I do?' is answered, 'do this!' and the only question that remains is 'how?'. For that it calls on experts and scientists, social and antisocial, learns how to take or ignore advice, and gets on with the job.

The crucial feature of this caricature is that it rests on a distinction between fact and value judgment, identifies the setting of a purpose or end with the latter, and supposes that it reduces the subsequent task to that of technical implementation. Whatever usefulness there may be in the fact-value or means-ends distinctions—although careful analysis finds these far from as simple as is often supposed—they do not support this neat separation of tribunal functions. It is a serious mistake to suppose that some tribunals are merely purpose-setting and others simply purpose-implementing. All tribunals inescapably have, in varying degree, both tasks. And in addition, all are involved in another baffling activity which I shall call the 'interpretation' of purpose.

Purposes, however specific, usually do not come isolated or discrete. Preventing floods is a clear enough purpose. So is improving navigation. So is developing hydro-electric power. But all are in the field together, along with a host of others: helping the small farmer, and encouraging the efficient big farmer, and reducing surpluses, and encouraging private power companies, and developing public power, and providing recreational areas, etc. Building a dam here will prevent floods. But what of its effect on this or that other purpose? Why not a dam there instead? Or three little ones? Or one really big one plus a canal? The selection of means to achieve any particular purpose is fraught with consequences for other purposes. The weighing of these is inseparably related to choosing means, and father has no time for all these perplexities. The implementing tribunal in its choice of means is deciding priority of purposes and cannot help but 'make policy.' This is not improper encroachment but unavoidable necessity, and we do better to recognize and train for it than to live with myths of impossible separation. My point is simply that, without challenging the means-ends distinction, the selection of means in any real situation involves judgments about the relative importance of purposes and that therefore the implementing tribunal is of necessity also a purpose-selecting or evaluating tribunal. The agent cannot be merely a technician.

But beyond the difficulties posed by the multiplicity of public purposes, even within a single tribunal, there are more. We can speak of a purpose or end as relatively clear and specific and think of reaching it as we think of solving a problem, riddle, or puzzle or even of winning a game. This problem-solving, goal-winning activity presupposes a 'given' end so given that we at least can know if the solution is found or the game is won. But 'having a problem' is not usually like this. 'Doctor,' runs the bitter jest, 'what's my problem?'

What is sometimes called a 'problematic situation' has this feature, paradoxical as it seems, of being simultaneously involved in the determination of means and the specification of ends. This means, put in terms appropriate to this discussion, that the purpose given a tribunal needs interpretation. And the suitability or 'rightness' of interpretation poses problems far more difficult than the question of the suitability of the selection of means.

The purposes with which our public tribunals are entrusted run a wide gamut, involving many levels of generality. Develop nuclear energy, maintain an adequate defensive system, regulate interstate commerce, carry out a national transportation policy, eliminate unfair labor practices, establish and administer a state university, develop a fair rent structure, regulate television in the public interest— these are a miscellaneous few out of thousands. In one sense, they tell the tribunal what to do. But it would surely be a mistake to say that all the tribunal needs to do is to figure out 'how'—to select the means. For meaningful as the statement of purpose may be there is still a need for an activity that we call by such terms as explicating, defining, refining or narrowing, specifying, concretizing, spelling out: a range that I cover with the notion of interpreting.

Since the problem of interpretation is prominent also in the casuistic mood I defer its analysis until later. Here I wish only to stress the fact that in our purposive or pragmatic mood we are confronted with inherent features of purpose which prevent the reduction of the purposive activity of tribunals to the purely instrumental, implementing, means-seeking, non-value-considering model. Both the interrelated multiplicity of relatively specific purposes and the inescapable generality of statements of purpose require, whether as weighing or interpreting, activity which must be classed as policy-making.

The Casuistic Mood

In any situation in which men are required to square their actions with principles, rules, or laws, whether these are embodied in a moral code, a political constitution, or legal regulations, a form of activity develops which, for want of a better name—and almost any other name would be a better name—might be called casuistry. I shall use the term without the invidious sense which Pascal's *Provincial Letters* fastened on it, expressing the inevitable outrage of the fundamentalist, strict-constructionist, against the lax or liberal construction of his more accommodating colleagues. Strict and liberal are two styles of the same art; and the art, which is casuistry, is simply the art of applying rules to concrete cases.

We tend, perhaps, to be impatient with the demand for 'principled' action; principles are always slowing us down. But a society raised on the Ten Commandments, the Bill of Rights, and the Rule of Law must learn to live with them. Our actions, private as well as public, are subject to the demand for 'justification' which, as often as not, is the demand that the act be squared with the relevant rule— whether it be 'Thou shalt not kill' or 'Congress shall make no law . . . abridging the freedom of speech.' Concern with this kind of justification is a pervasive aspect of social life. For the public agent, acting within a carefully erected framework of authorization and law, the concern is pressing and inescapable; as an agent of law as well as of purpose he is inevitably, without disparagement, a casuist.

The myth—and there is one here too—is that the well-behaved tribunal enforces or implements the law without stretching, or interpreting what is given; that this is a technical task which can be done without invading the law-making or policy sphere. But this myth also encounters two obstacles. First, the multiplicity of laws, however specific, provides a variety of premises, supporting different conclusions, among which choice is required. Second, rules contain general terms which need definition or specification. 'Congress shall make no law respecting an establishment of religion' means something. But does it mean that Congress shall favor no particular church or does it mean that it cannot aid religion impartially? Something is given in the law; the constitution is not a *tabula rasa*. But what does it mean? Enforcement requires decision about meaning, and it is difficult to know whether the specification of meaning—interpretation—could best be described as 'discovering' or 'giving' meaning. Choice and interpretation are an inseparable part of the applying or enforcing of law, and this makes impossible a mechanical or merely technical performance of the law-applying function. That this is not universally understood can be seen in the reaction to the Supreme Court's decision in the school case. The fourteenth amendment requires 'equal protection.' Does that mean 'separate but equal' or does it mean 'non-segregated'? Is holding one a policy invasion while holding the other is not? Or is the choice a choice between policies so that either choice is a policy choice. In that case what becomes of the view that applying the constitution, 'saying what it means,' does not involve policy decisions? And what, then, is the Court? These are familiar and perplexing questions and they turn upon the nature of the art of interpretation.

But casuistry is not at work only in courts. Every tribunal which operates in a context of law finds itself involved in these problems.

The Interplay of Purpose and Law

While the dominance of purpose or of law gives to deliberation a pragmatic or a casuistic flavor, purpose and law are closely related and I wish to point out some general features of their interplay within the tribunal.

We should not take as more than suggestive a theory of stages through which institutions must develop, but in a tentative spirit, and taking a clue from Sir Henry Maine, I take a step in the direction of historical mythology. Speaking of the development of legal institutions Maine suggests a movement from an initial stage of justice without law to a stage of strict law to a stage of equity or interpretation. The first stage could be described as 'purpose dominated.' The existence of a kind of social problem leads to the creation of a tribunal which is given a purpose expressed in such terms as 'promote justice.' Case after case requires interpretation of what 'justice' demands, and the accumulation of cases, rulings, precedents results in the development of a body of law which stands as the 'explication' or 'embodiment' or 'spelling out' of justice. Gradually, appeals to the tribunal shift from appeals to the purpose, i.e. 'Justice demands . . .' to appeals to the law, i.e. 'The law requires . . .'; and we reach the stage of 'rule-domination,' or strict law, in which the purpose of the tribunal seems to be to enforce the law. But life moves on and we become aware of a growing disparity between the demands of the law and of justice. The law which once seemed to spell out justice seems now to have misspelled it, legality seems to move apart from morality or justice. As this sense develops we find ourselves appealing from the law to justice, to the half-forgotten but reawakening purpose of the tribunal. At this stage we reshape the law through various devices, chiefly perhaps through interpretation, and liberal interpretation at that, stretching the letter to the spirit or the purpose.

This, in crude form, is Maine's tale, and I am not concerned with its general historical accuracy. It does, however, fit the development of many of our public tribunals: a felt need, an agency with a vague, general purpose, the slow development of a web of rules spelling out the meaning of the purpose, the changing character of deliberation from the pragmatic to the casuistic mood, the reinterpretation of the rules in the light of new interpretations of the purpose. But whether this is the history of a particular tribunal or not, the story puts its finger on the interplay of purpose and law. The case for a law is, after all, its bearing on a purpose, whether by way of implementation or explication. Purpose gets embodied in law. And law, when we interpret it is reshaped in the light of purpose. This is not only a matter of general stages; the interplay of purpose and law is pervasive.

But the 'stage' idea is suggestive at another point. Putting aside the temporal theme, let us imagine a scale or spectrum marked at one end 'rule-dominated' and at the other end 'purpose-dominated.' Taking as our clue the character of argument before or within it—as predominantly an appeal to law or to purpose—tribunals can be roughly located on the scale. Thus, to no one's surprise, the judicial tribunals find themselves at the rule-dominated end of the scale, facing the demand that every decision be in accordance with a pre-existing rule. At the other end of the scale, purpose-dominated, we find the 'sovereign tribunal,' the amending power, and, moving in slightly, our legislative tribunals. Out of neatness I place the administrative tribunals in the middle range, the younger ones like the Atomic Energy Commission toward the purposive end, the older ones like the I.C.C. toward the rule-dominated end.

The traditional classification of tribunals into Legislative, Administrative, and Judicial seems to me to be less revealing of a tribunal's character than placing it on the rule-purpose scale. Obviously the I.C.C. is more like a court than it is like the A.E.C. in what it does, and in the habit of mind required of the agent. We can also describe 'rule of law' demands such as expressed in the Uniform Administrative Procedure Act as the demand of lawyers that young tribunals behave according to procedures that make sense at the rule-bound end of the scale, the lawyers' natural habitat.

Certain theoretical questions adjust themselves to this scheme in fairly revealing ways. For example, at the rule-bound end we encounter not only the conception of the rule of law but the question of whether 'rule-bound' can possibly extend to the removal of all discretion in a mechanical theory of jurisprudence. At the other end, the sovereign tribunal encounters the theory of natural law and the assertion that even the highest tribunal within a system, the most purposive, is still operating in a context of law which the tribunal did not create and which limits its authority.

Certain correlations stand out. As we move from one end to the other we move also from predictability to flexibility or predictability to arbitrariness, depending on one's concern. We also move from the dominance of the interpretive arts to the dominance of the predictive arts (or science). And we also find that the more rule-bound the tribunal is, the less we are concerned to maintain its 'popular' character.

But enough of this. I turn from these suggestions growing out of the interplay of purpose and law to a consideration of some of the more paradoxical aspects of the art of interpretation, required, as I have argued, in both the pragmatic and the casuistic moods of tribunal deliberation.

The Paradox of Interpretation

'Interpretation' is a notion of great significance, but it is also terribly baffling. Its paradoxical character arises from its involvement with pairs of apparently opposed notions which it tries, without denying the opposition, to reconcile. 'Finding' and 'making,' 'discovering' and 'creating,' 'the same' and 'different' seem obviously opposed to each other. What, then, of the insistence of the interpreter that his making is only finding, his creating only discovering, and that the new product is only the same thing after all? The temptation is to say, 'nothing!' Finding is finding; making is making. Let us not confuse what is distinct. And undoubtedly there are situations in which confusion is uncalled for. We do not make the mountains we may find on the other side of the moon, nor the penny we find on the walk. Let us accept this ordinary distinction without pushing into the 'philosophical' issue of the phenomenal world as itself a product of mind, so that we are always discovering our own creature. At the penny-finding level, creating and discovering are two different things. But even at this level there are situations which demand some subtlety.

An architect is called in by a family to design their house. They tell him what they need or want. He produces the plan. Is that it? Exactly! (Some architect! Some family!) How should we describe this process? The architect was told what to do, and he did it. But, on the other hand, he was not told what to do. He did something, and the product was greeted with recognition. Recognition? Is this the plan you had in mind? Yes, of course not! You have discovered exactly what I wanted. Or rather, you have created exactly what I want. The dream house never quite seen in my dreams. The architect is an 'interpreter.' Did he create or discover? Did he carry out orders? Yes and no.

An actor interprets Hamlet. A great interpretation! What Shakespeare had in mind? Or should have had in mind, or *really* had in mind? A great discovery? A new creation? Shakespeare's or not?

Or a student gropes for expression. 'Is this what you mean?' 'Yes, that's it.' But is it really? Did you discover what he had in mind or did you put something there? The 'recognition' is real enough. That is what he meant to say; although it is also the case that he did not know what he meant to say.

Or we explicite 'cause'; we offer an interpretation. Presumably the interpretation 'means the same' as what is interpreted. But it does not look the same and I may be surprised at what I am told I mean. Is this a new proposal? Partly, but not really. It only clears things up. But 'clearing up' is itself a confusing notion. How can I end up clearer and still mean the same thing?

These scattered examples are of familiar interpretive situations and they can, no doubt, be taken firmly in hand and cleaned up, ambiguity and paradox removed. But it is more important, I think, to absent ourselves from felicity awhile and tolerate paradox while we reflect on the strange intermingling of discovering and creating, the same and the different, in 'interpreting.'

The key to the situation lies in the fact that the interpreter is not on his own. It is not his house or his play or his confusion he is going to work on. He is, in fact, an agent, acting for another, transforming what is given, but in the name of the giver. The interpreter of meaning finds, or tries to find, the meaning that is *there*; but he seems also to be putting it there. If the first seems more appropriate to his role, the second seems better to describe his actions. But the interpreter is not a free agent; his work is judged in special terms. 'Very good,' we might say, 'but not what is called for.' It is the fact of agency which limits creativeness by the demand for discovery. The Supreme Court interprets the constitution. Is it discovering its meaning or giving it meaning? The difficulties in which the political interpreter is involved are the same difficulties as are posed for all interpretive activity: for the artist, the philosophical analyst, the interpreter of dreams and parables, as well as for the public agent, the interpreter of the public will.

I touch only briefly on the form taken by the problem of interpretation for the political agent. First, as the interpreter of purpose, the agent finds himself dealing with aims, desires, interests, goals more or less generally or vaguely expressed. These he must interpret, as the architect interprets the vague desires of his client. He is carrying out the 'will of the people,' but this will is no more discoverable in a public opinion poll, for example, than the plan of the house is found in the scratchy hints the architect is handed.

If he is indeed the agent of the public will, it is of an inarticulate will which he must interpret, with all the shaping creativity that requires.

Second, as an interpreter of the law, whether constitutional enactment or legislative act, he is involved in giving to or finding meaning in general statements. The agent of the lawgiver, he is necessarily involved in discovering his 'intent.' But every student of the court knows what this involves. The meaning is not there to be found by simply looking or asking. But something is there which bears on the appropriateness of the meaning declared. The study of interpretation in the casuistic mood is complex and fascinating. It is best pursued in the study of our Supreme Court. I regret that I cannot pursue the matter here.

Guided as he is by the tribunal context the public agent is inescapably an interpreter of purpose and of law. It is only in myth that making is reduced to finding, creating to asking. As an agent, he has a task; he also has discretion. But if the discretion is, as I have argued, more than discretion in implementing, if it is also interpretive discretion, then the whole structure of consent, authorization, or delegation takes on a new look and, as I indicated in an earlier chapter, the compatibility of delegation with self-government is called into question. The dilemma is easier to state than to resolve. To see the representative or agent as the servant doing what we tell him, simply carrying out our detailed wishes or orders, is to insure the disaster born of ignorance. To see him as authorized to be creative on behalf of the body politic, to be the interpreter of the general will makes our anti-authoritarian hackles rise. But this, in the end, is what he must be. And this is why I have lingered so long, with such sympathy for paradox over the concept of interpretation, with its double aspect. For it is only the retained sense of 'discovery' which keeps the authorization of 'creativity' from being simply a case of abdication to the unguided will and insight of a master.

THE GUARDIAN AGENT

And so, at long last, seeing the public agent more as interpreter than servant, we grope our way back to the *Republic* and join Plato in the search for the guardian type, for the agent who by endowment and the training of mind and character can play the public role. But at the door of this mansion we pause for a moment to look back at the desperate attempt to shun the house of Plato as if it were the lair of Circe. We are coming to the end of the attempt to find salvation in competition and machinery, in the offsetting clash of countervailing power, in the lame schoolboy wisdom of Federalist 10 warped into a democratic credo. 'Who will guard the guardian?' we say, as we proceed to set a thief to catch a thief. 'Who is to judge?' Every man has a right to his opinion, and one opinion is as good as another. Therefore, lay about you! Not our wisdom, not our character or discipline, but the 'process' will save us, transforming (without reforming us) our private vices into public virtues.

It is the pathetic hope of this familiar view that only thus can 'democracy' be saved. 'Wisdom' and 'character' smack of aristocracy and lead us to 'elitism.' To make all men good and wise seems beyond hope. What is left, then, but to construct a theory of government which does not require these rarities? And here it is at hand: the marketplace, self-interest, and an easier set of virtues, every man his own agent, monopoly the only real disease.

But it will not do. The heedless city has been saved by a saving remnant, by quiet intelligence and devotion, not by brawling bustle and random energy. I do not give up on democracy, but I do not see how we can save it by weakening or corrupting the conception of the public agent to less than that combination of wisdom, character, and power to which Plato, almost in despair, gave the name 'Philosopher-King.'

The basic questions are still those of the *Republic:* Is there a guardian type? How can he be found or recruited? How can he be educated for his function? How can we delay his corruption?

No one who has taught in the fields of political theory or philosophy or 'citizenship' can avoid the impression, disturbing though it may be, that there is a guardian type, the perceptive responsibility-bearer. Even if it is assumed that all men have latent capacity in this direction, there are some who seem to be 'naturals.' They come from everywhere, from any and every class and background, and they are pearls beyond price for the recruiter.

It is here, at the stage of recruitment, that we must face the problem of the love of power and the old truth that those who love power cannot be trusted with it. We are oddly ambivalent at this point. We like our candidate to be reluctant, Cincinnatus dragged from the plow. But still, he must fight for his place and want it. We tend to confuse leadership with dominance. To dominate is to succeed in mastering a situation, to impose one's own interests. Leadership, however, is quite unlike this. The leader is one who, curbing his 'own' interests, makes himself the effective champion of the interest of the enterprise, the spokesman or agent of the community. To be dominant, power-loving, assertive, is to be unfit for the guardian role. We have tried hard to make it a virtue, but ambition is at best only a usable vice. It is less the case that power corrupts than that the power-seeking type is a corrupted counterfeit of the public agent and, when he wins authority, reveals his fundamental corruption. The love of power, as Plato saw, is not the mark of the guardian. If all this seems like nonsense, it is not, I make bold to assert, that Plato is wrong, but that we are pretty far gone.

The educating of the public agent for his function presents us with even greater difficulties than does recruiting. And now too, as in Greece, the Sophist hangs up his sign and offers the ten-drachma course, the quick way, the short-cut to winning friends and influencing people, techniques packed in clichés—how to govern without wisdom. Alas, there is no short-cut. But, on the other hand, why the hurry? Must we always be so busy putting out fires in the attic that we cannot attend to the sinking foundation?

Even without haste, education seems to present us with insoluble problems. There are so many facts, fields, disciplines. It is relatively easy to train a specialist. With a little more time and effort we can turn out a man who is narrow in more than a single field. Even this, however, does not add up to the desired wisdom and we still seek the key to education that is 'general' or 'coherent' or 'integrated.' But these notions have gotten us nowhere. They do little more than express dissatisfaction with education that is too specialized, incoherent, and fragmentary; they remind us that our current administration of knowledge makes the cultivation of intelligence difficult, that a modern university is not an educational institution and that it makes a shambles of the college. In this situation it is almost with relief that we greet the graduate who has emerged with a clear, hard specialty and with an unimpaired mind.

But when we remember the agent as the 'interpreter' the situation begins to seem hopeless indeed. How can we educate for *that*? How can we produce creative interpreters of a culture? I wish I knew. There is no course for this in the college catalogue. But if there is a division of the college that holds the key it is the division of the Humanities, with the immersion it can provide in the arts, the literature and poetry, the religious, moral, and philosophical reflection through which the mind and spirit of a culture seek expression. The social sciences are necessary; but they are no substitute for the Humanities even if they include, under the mantle of anthropology, the culture concept. But this, I am sure, is not the sort of remedy we are willing to embrace. A quick embrace perhaps, but not the necessary marriage.

But what about 'ethics'? Ethical theory is, of course, concerned with human conduct and with certain features of choice and decision. It is concerned generally with values, principles, and method which, in the political context, have been discussed here as purpose, law, and procedure. But a course in ethics is not a short course in practical wisdom, and it is more likely to deepen perplexity than to turn one loose with answers.

There are, of course, moral problems at several levels for which there are 'answers.' Like everyone else, the public agent should not steal or take bribes. If this is news to the agent there has been a mistake somewhere. But beyond this there are institutional mores involving loyalty upward and downward, the manners of disagreement and resignation, all kinds of cases of conscience—the ethics, in short, of a profession. On the whole, we look to the institution to develop and guard and to impress these upon the initiate. But even beyond this, and most significantly, we reach the

evaluative activity inherent in interpretation, and here
ethical theory, and reflection, is only, along with the
Humanities generally, a part of the soil which nourishes
but does not answer. Ethical theory is to creative moral or
political action as aesthetic theory is to the work of the
artist.

The education of the ruler, of the political agent, is still
our greatest unmet educational challenge. It is, I have suggested, the central theme, if not the lost chord, of 'liberal'
education. The theory of education is essentially the theory
of the government of mind; it is hopeless when it is not at
the same time a theory of the state—a theory of political
obligation.

Finally, how can we forestall corruption? The selection
and the training of the agent is, of course, the crucial safeguard. And beyond individual integrity we count on the
supporting vigilance of the corps and its 'esprit.' Can we
do more? Plato's ascetic way of life for the guardian—no
family, no private property—seems to us too extreme a way
of avoiding the conflict of interest situation. Our shepherds
have flocks within the flock.

'We must watch the guardians,' we say. 'They must
answer to us.' But who guards the guardian's guardian?
Somewhere the regress ends and we rest on the unwatched
watcher. There, in the end, we must depend on character.
Ours?

And what of our favorite device—the dispersion of power,
the quest for safety in weakness? To this, the world now
gives its answer. The work that government must do takes
strength, sureness, vigor, confidence. Such power gone
astray is a terrible menace. But to attempt to safeguard
virtue by the creation of impotence is to lose everything.

4

Democracy

If I had to select a figure of speech which, upon analysis, would reveal the basic dilemma of our political life, I would choose the 'marketplace of ideas.' 'The best test of truth,' one of our sages has told us, 'is the power of the thought to get itself accepted in the competition of the market.' (How I wish some genius had thrown equal light on another dark area of our lives by proclaiming that the best test of virtue is 'the power of a desire to get itself accepted in the competition of the market.' But we must work with what we have and regretfully I leave the marketplace of virtue and take up my drier theme.)

The marketplace of ideas! Do we appreciate enough the revolutionary daring of that conception? At one bold stroke it identifies the deliberative and the bargaining arts, turns the scientist into a businessman, the sage into the salesman. This is the most significant triumph of a business civilization. Or it would be, if it did not ensure disaster. For, unfortunately, we need the product of deliberation, and, however difficult it may be for us to recapture the sense of difference, deliberating and bargaining are not the same, neither in process nor in result. Education turns on this difference. The school, said one of the Popes, is either a Temple or a Den. It is, I would agree, either the nurturer of

the deliberative animal or, failing that, a bordello of the
mind. *idealism ⇒ popular*

The aristocratic theory of government, whatever its shortcomings in practice, also rests upon this distinction. It sees
governing as a difficult art or profession requiring a high
order of intelligence, discipline, and character. Its basic
assertion is that only a few are capable of meeting the demands of this form of deliberative life. The democrat,
when democracy was a creed that mattered, did not disagree about the difficulty of governing. He argued, rather,
that all (or most) men have deliberative and moral poten-
tiality and that given the proper education and environment, each could take his place in the deliberative forum
and share the responsibilities of sovereignty. And why
should he do this? Not simply in order to get more, but
primarily in order to develop his deliberative and moral
character and to achieve the dignity of being a ruler of the
society of which he is a member. For this is the genuine
democratic urge, impervious to all the cornucopias of the
most benevolent paternalism.

With both misgivings and hopes we gingerly extended
the franchise and launched into mass education. But where
is the optimist today who has not shaken his head over
apathy and private preoccupation, over the growing complexity of public issues, over the shortcomings of public
education, and the mind-destroying uses of mass communication. Have we not been brought, if we think about these
matters, to consider again whether the life of politics is
indeed the life for everyone, whether there are not also
other paths than the political to dignity and self-realization?

The essential feature of a democratic polity is its concern for the participation of the member in the process by
which the community is governed. It goes beyond the in-

sistence that politics or government be included among the careers open to talent. It gives to each citizen a public office, a place in the sovereign tribunal and, unless it is a sham, it places its destiny in the hands of that tribunal. Here is the ultimate decision-maker, the court of last appeal, the guardian of the guardians, government 'by the people.'The significance of democracy as an ideal rests on the significance of participation in the sovereign tribunal; for the democrat, being tribunal-worthy is what being a rational animal means, and the character we bring to the office of the citizen is the crucial test of culture. It is not clear that we are passing that test.

It is altogether possible that we may drift increasingly in the direction of ritualistic democracy. We will feel little pain and the portrait of Lincoln will not come crashing from the wall. But popular participation in politics may become increasingly meaningless, popular mandates increasingly directionless, as we seek to protect the 'responsible' institutions of government from the effects of mindless participation and clamor. Without too much imagination we can see the Presidential Sweepstakes becoming the main event, combining the excitement of a national lottery with the thrill of a coronation. We will redouble our efforts and turn out the votes, but the vote will decide less and less as we move deeper into the morass of public relations, the projection of images, and the painless engineering of consent. Perhaps this path is inevitable for us, but it is not democracy—only its tragic parody.

The alternative is difficult indeed. It demands the reshaping of the electorate into a genuinely deliberative tribunal capable of dealing responsibly with fundamental issues. It would require vastly more and better education than we have yet been able to achieve, and would require a revolution in our habits and institutions of communication. We would need to transform ourselves from domestic into political animals. The task seems overwhelming.

It is here, as we gird ourselves for heroic effort, that the temptation appears—not the aristocratic temptation to which the Grand Inquisitor succumbed but a temptation which parades itself as democratic. It is the temptation of the marketplace. Why, it whispers, dream of impossible tribunals manned by thoughtful, devoted, disinterested *laziness* angels deliberating about the common good. There is a better plan, which takes men as they are and asks of them only what is possible and pleasant. We know this story well: the unleashing of competitiveness, the guiltless assertion of self-interest, the eternal selling of everything— our products and services, our programs and ideas, ourselves. Why man a tribunal when we can have a market instead? Come, let us bargain together.

It would be a major task to trace and assess the impact of the marketplace upon our culture. I cannot be concerned here even with the broad range of its effect upon our political life. But the attempt to understand the problems of political democracy in America today involves us inescapably in the struggle between the life of the marketplace and the life of the forum or tribunal.

We do not, of course, hear much of this struggle in our public education. The received doctrine beds down the lion with the lamb. But our attempts at education for democracy, for participation in public life, are hopelessly perplexed by the divergent demands of marketplace and tribunal. How, for example, shall we teach our children to communicate with the necessary respect for the integrity of language, and for each other, when we support (almost as culture heroes) a large class of professional liars to hail with impartial sincerity the claim of any client? This is not intended as a 'personal' remark; the point is precisely that advertising is a respectable profession in our marketplace culture. But how, supporting such a profession, can we really make the point that the integrity of communication is the wellspring of a community's life? It is no answer to say that we have learned to defend ourselves by not believing what we hear, or that propaganda will counter propaganda and the truth will prevail even though no one tells it. We are poisoning the wells, and we cannot live on antidotes.

Add to our prevailing style of communication the familiar emphasis on individualism, private interest, and private enterprise and the story of our education for democracy is almost told. We teach men to compete and bargain. Are we to be surprised, then, at the corruption of the tribunal into its marketplace parody?

Democratic political life turns upon the office of the citizen and upon the demands of that office. The citizen is, in his political capacity, a public agent with all that that implies. He is asked public, not private questions: 'Do we need more public schools?' not 'Would I like to pay more taxes?'. He must, in this capacity, be concerned with the public interest, not with his private goods. His communication must be colleagial, not manipulative. He must deliberate, not bargain. This is the program. And it is simply the application of tribunal manners to the electoral tribunal. Nothing is more certain than that the abandonment of this conception spells the doom of meaningful democracy.

And we are abandoning it. But do we care? We prosper. More people have more things and give thanks in more churches than ever before. Our complex political institutions operate. This, at long last, seems to be it. Here and there a critic strikes a mild Veblenian note (and we chuckle with him), or bemoans the lonely crowd, the organization man, the road to Miltown, the move to the suburbs, the rise in mental ills. But for these critics we have a delicious phrase—merchants of doom and gloom—and we are not buying any.

The voice of doom needs to be louder before we hear it. Apparently it speaks Russian. In the 'thirties the social critic spoke against the background of internal economic collapse. For the 'fifties, and perhaps the 'sixties, the Russians take the place of unemployment. The test is 'will it solve them?'. It is an external standard which leaves the quality of our own lives out of the picture. But it is a convenient test. Enough scientists and engineers is simply 'more than they have'; the right rate of capital investment is 'more than theirs.' Ominous statistics seem now to threaten free-enterprise as nothing else has. We are, sporadically, shaken by glimpses of the future. But we do very little.

In these cold war circumstances the prospects for the revitalization of the popular tribunal are rather slim. We seem, in fact, to be giving up even on the hope that our legislative bodies will be able to transform themselves from bargaining assemblies into competent policy-making tribunals and turn more and more to the Executive for salvation. But if the outcome is some form of ritualistic or plebescitic democracy let us not put the blame too quickly on human nature or on the Russians. For our own ideas will have done more than anything else to corrupt the popular tribunal and turn the hope of democratic government to ashes. We will, I hope, soon learn that it is bootless to drive the money-changer from the Temple only to let him set up shop in the Forum.

Let me deal briefly with some of the conceptions or mis-
conceptions which plague us.

That Government should give us what we want.

The contrast between what we want and what is good for
us is certainly familiar enough. Every child knows the force
of this distinction and, no doubt, looks forward to the day
of freedom when he can at last do what he wants. But
parental, and social, authority exerts itself to ensure that
by the time the child moves out to govern his own life he
too will honor by observance the contrast between what
he wants and what he thinks best.

The relation between 'good' and 'desire' is the oldest
theme of moral reflection, and it is still a lively theme.
Variations run from the complete identification of good
and desire to complete separation, and it would be pointless
to be dogmatic here. It is difficult, however, to see how the
conception of 'good' for an animal, of whatever kind, can
avoid ultimate involvement with his needs, wants, desires.
But at the same time not even a wholehearted hedonism
can quite deny that indulging a particular desire at some
particular time might be bad. Even if the good is taken as
happiness, happiness as pleasure, pleasure as the satisfaction
of desire, it is still the case that the satisfaction of a particular desire may turn out not to be good. In one way or another we come to recognize that immediacy or urgency is
not a sufficient guide, that impulse may need checking, and
that, at times, there is a difference between what we happen
to want and what is good for us. Governing ourselves is not
doing what we want; it is doing what we think best.

This is no less the case for our political lives. Government
is purposive, but it is a mistake to suppose that its purpose
is simply to give us what we want, to conform its action

to what happens at any particular time to be the state of popular feeling or desire. Political tribunals, including the ✓ electorate, are not simply clumsy, pre-scientific devices for determining the state of community desire; nor, in intention, are they the servants of that desire, even if it could be determined. We recognize this when we reserve our greatest admiration for the statesman, who seldom gives us what we want, and condemn the politician who fails to do what is needed because of 'public opinion.'

We mislead ourselves when we talk of government as the servant of the people. What, in a democracy, can that mean? Whose servant is the electorate? And what are we supposed to give ourselves? A democracy had better take as its slogan: 'It is not the aim of government to give us what we want.' It needs this reminder more than it needs an urge to self-indulgence. Government is not the tool of our impulsiveness but the instrument of our deliberate selves; it is people doing as they think best, and this is not always 'what they want.'

But here we see the divergent tendencies of the forum and the marketplace. Our schools, if they do their work, strengthen our deliberate and deliberative selves. Between the impression and the conviction, between the impulse and the action we learn to pause and to consider. But out of school we spend enormous sums to undo this work. We advertise. We put our knowledge of the mind to work against reflection, to make the impression deeper and indelible, to trigger impulse into action. The teacher and the salesman are the deadliest of enemies, one fighting to strengthen, the other to weaken, the human mind.

The product of advertising, we are told, is 'consumer demand.' And what is that but public opinion or the will of the people? In making us see the 'will of the people' as a version of consumer demand, popular sovereignty as consumer sovereignty, the marketplace view of life strikes a fundamental blow at the conception of self-government. It transforms the citizen from ruler to consumer and substitutes for the habits of responsibility the arts of acquisition and enjoyment.

That self-interested competition between individuals, interests, and factions promotes the general good.

This popular creed is not unrelated to what has just been mentioned. Its significance for us here lies in what it does to the popular tribunal. It boldly converts what has generally been regarded as political disease into the model of proper political function, harnessing the power of private vice to the chariot of public virtue. Or so it is hoped. How deep is our conviction that in pursuing each his own interest, merging for greater effectiveness into interest-groups, we are acting as moral agents of the public weal. Oh, kindly invisible hand who has made virtue so easy! Each knows what he wants and labels it 'good' and chases it. And all the little goods add up to one great big public good. We run for fun and make the treadmill go.

Self-interest and competitiveness are ancient facts of life and not the inventions of political theorists. But there is something novel and bold in seeing them not as tendencies to be curbed but as powers to be encouraged and harnessed. The case we have made for competitive individualism is familiar enough; it has two main features.

First, it is claimed that to encourage competition is to spur individuals to greater creative effort to heighten their energies, develop their powers and skills, and, in general, to increase the quantity and raise the quality of human achievement.

And second, it is held that the energies thus released are essentially self-corrective in their operation, that excesses are offset, and that a competitive system has inherent balance and moves in a desirable direction. Progress, in short, through conflict; the competitor the agent of progress.

There is little doubt that competition is a spur. We are so imbued with its spirit that we find it difficult to imagine another motive for effort and achievement. We think of the desire to achieve as the desire to succeed, the desire to succeed as the desire to surpass others, to win the race, to climb to the top. No one, I suppose, has had a keener eye for our emulative proclivities than Veblen but, as he pointed out, there is, besides the desire to master others, the desire to master tasks or problems, the sense of craftsmanship. The craving to excel others is only a corrupt form of the craving for excellence.

But competition is a cheap source of motive power, and we can turn almost anything into a competitive sport. We can turn 'learning' into competition for grades; but we should not be surprised if the victims grow into competitors without a love for learning. Competition, in short, produces competitors. But competitiveness is as likely to be an obstacle as a spur to genuine creativity. We need, I think, to re-examine the assumption that the energies released by self-interested competition are productive of excellence. The conception of life as a competitive game is not the profoundest conception of the human situation.

As for the self-regulating features of a competitive system, the belief in which gives to the competitor the moral assurance that he is still playing a necessary social role as he looks out for himself—this is, of course, an echo of the metaphysical optimism expressed in doctrines of evolution through natural selection and of the inevitability of progress. The massive growth of regulation, however, testifies to the end of general faith in non-regulation. And, in any case, the staunchest believer in 'fitness will flourish' can have nothing to object to in the spectacle of the flourishing of government. Faith in factionalism is, I believe, dying out, and although we sometimes give ourselves the dialectical reassurance that every power contains within itself the seeds of its own countervailing power, our hopes rest increasingly not upon the matched giants in the marketplace but upon the institutions of the 'public sector.'

Still, competitive individualism lingers as a creed and partly shapes our character. To the extent that this is the case we man the public tribunal with a spirit alien to its demands and find ourselves acting the ruler with the manners of the marketplace. Invited to co-operative deliberation we respond with competitive bargaining.

That compromise is a reasonable and democratic way of dealing with controversy.

The roots of the doctrine of compromise go deep and it would, I think, be a mistake to treat it simply as—what it nevertheless is—the marketplace conception of 'being reasonable.' It draws its theoretical strength from cognitive skepticism and what used to be called moral or ethical relativism. To claim infallibility is to take the path of fanaticism; to impose our own values on others makes us zealots and tyrants. Fanatics and zealots are always at each other's throats and unless they mend their ways the issue comes to force and war. So we must begin with the recognition that our beliefs and our values are only 'ours,' overcome vanity and self-righteousness, and acknowledge that those who disagree with us about what we believe in or cherish most deeply are not necessarily fools or scoundrels but mortals caught up, as we are, in the inevitable partialities and limitations of the human animal.

Some such views as these (dare we say truths?) lie behind the defense of compromise. How can we resolve our differences when the assurance of cognitive or moral certitude is only an illusion fathered by a wish? Nor can we appeal to an 'arbitrary' standard if all do not accept it as the arbiter. What, then, can we do but seek accommodation, give and take, strike a bargain and accept it with good grace? To do this is to be modest, tolerant, skeptical, sociable, civilized, humane, reasonable. Otherwise we are arrogant, intolerant, dogmatic, anti-social, barbaric, inhumane, irrational. This should do to suggest the division of persons into those with whom we can do business and those beyond the pale, the compromising and the uncompromising.

Unfortunately, the doctrine fails us in several respects. It does not seem to apply where things really matter; nor does it produce anything really satisfactory. It is, as a political doctrine, a sort of weary congressional view of things. It may 'contain' conflict and quiet the House but it contains very little else, and certainly does not contain the art of governing.

Disagreement in belief and in attitude is a familiar fact of life, and we are all cognitive and moral security risks, or at least we cannot be sure who is not. But it does not follow from the recognition of our fallibility and partiality that our salvation lies in the compromise or the bargain. Where has it saved us or created what we value? Scientists disagree, but does science move by compromise? Is great art the product of compromise? Has compromise given Socrates or Jesus to the world—Crito and the Compromise on the Mount? Whom shall we advise to bargain? Is it for lovers or for friends, for families or colleagues, for priests or teachers? Bargaining is the death of any fellowship.

But what, then, shall we do? We come together and must decide and act; but we disagree. As we consider this situation we must recognize that it has two related but distinct aspects. First, there is the problem of holding the group or enterprise together in the face of disagreement which threatens disintegration. But second, there is the need to meet the problem or challenge with which the group is faced. There is thus both an internal and an external problem, and we must not lose sight of either.

When we think of problem-solving or decision-making as an individual matter our attention is usually focused on the external problem and on the adequacy of the solution. But when a group is confronted with a problem and its members disagree our attention is caught by this aspect of the situation and we become involved in group dynamics and 'inter-personal relations.' Saving the group becomes the problem with priority, and we nourish the arts of reducing heat, smoothing rough edges, and keeping everyone involved and happy. This is desirable and even necessary. It becomes dangerous, however, when we seek to achieve harmony by techniques which purchase this harmony at the expense of adequate solution of the external problem. Among them is the technique of compromise.

The case for compromise is that it is better than warfare and that it holds a group together. No one gets everything he wants but everyone gets something, and, getting something, is content to go along. This is, after all, what the bargaining transaction involves; each gives up something and each gets something. But how does cohesiveness thus purchased leave the external problem? Has the bargain solved it? The answer, unfortunately, is that it has not. The

result of the pulling and hauling, the gains and the con-
cessions, is all too often the elimination of just those elements of clarity, simplicity, imagination, and daring which
are needed. We never describe an improvement in a plan
as a compromise. Nor is a compromise the 'best that is
possible.' Everyone involved thinks that it is worse than
something else, and most are probably right. The only consolation is that it could be worse; it is a lesser evil as it is
also a lesser good. But, as Pascal pointed out, if the lesser
evil is a kind of good it is also true that a lesser good is a
kind of evil.

To approach decision in the bargaining spirit is to confuse
'solving' with 'getting.' This confusion is part of the pathol-
ogy of the governing process. It has the odd result of making
two heads worse than one, and it makes a committee utterly
hopeless. There is a place for bargaining in life, but it is an
imposter in the tribunal. To enshrine it, as the process of
compromise, in the political forum is to insure that the
political process will fail to meet its challenge and will indeed become a 'second best' way of dealing with secondary
issues. This is a degradation we cannot afford; if we fail
now in politics what else is there to turn to?

The art of common deliberation is not an easy one. It
calls on all the powers of the mind. It demands honesty,
courage, objectivity, and self-discipline in the presence of
passionate commitment. It is a co-operative not a competitive activity and, in spirit, utterly alien to the bargaining
temper of the marketplace.

But the belief in compromise goes hand in hand with the
belief in consumer sovereignty, competitive individualism,
and the invisible hand. And these are the notions which
have subverted the authentic conception of democratic

political life and brought us helpless and bemused into our age of anxiety—Hamlets in Supermarkets.

I do not argue, although I may seem to, that democracy demands the abdication of the private pursuit of private goods. But it does involve each of us in two discontinuous roles and this duality is the source of much perplexity. Plato, in the *Republic*, limits the governing function to a small class. To these rulers Plato does, so far as possible, deny a private life. The guardians have no private homes, no families, no private property. Those outside the ruling class, on the other hand, have only private lives. The rulers and the subjects constitute two separate classes and each class has its own way of life. The one does not meddle in politics; the other does nothing else. Each person has only a single role to play.

Marketplace democracy also, in its own way, gives to each person only a single role. For it asserts the essential continuity of private and public. The citizen is thought of primarily as a private person pursuing his own ends, and the political arena is only another setting for the same game. There, as elsewhere, each is the guardian of his own interests.

With both these forms of the denial of duality the authentic theory of democracy takes issue. Its basic assertion is that every citizen has two distinct roles to play. Each citizen is a member, a subject, a private person free within the common limits to pursue his own ends. But each is also an agent of the body politic, a ruler, a manner of the sovereign tribunal with all of the duties, obligations, and responsibilities that go with that role. It is the confusion of these roles which troubles us today.

We are familiar enough with the 'conflict of interest' situation and, in the case of ordinary tribunals, quite concerned to protect the public function against the intrusion of private distraction. But the office of the citizen is harder to protect. John Stuart Mill expressed reservations about the wisdom of the secret ballot. He feared that in its protective darkness men might be tempted to favor their private interests and come to regard the franchise as a private opportunity, forgetting that it is a public office. It is this sense of public office that we need most to recapture. Why are we indignant when someone sells his vote for a few dollars? Has he behaved any better if he sells or betrays it to his private self?

Internal conflict is inevitable since we have public roles as well as private lives. We must be disinterested while we are involved, objective where we are interested parties. And democratic government is not helped by theories which obscure or deny the duality of our situation and dissolve public duties into private privileges. We need, rather, a clearer view of the electoral tribunal, of the people acting, as Alexander Meiklejohn has taught us, as The Fourth Branch of Government. As a member of that Fourth—and basic—Branch the citizen must learn to move within a framework of ideas and habits appropriate to the ultimate agent of the body politic.

The theory and practice of The Fourth Branch is crucial to the life of a democracy. But the difficulty here is a strange one. The problem is not that of introducing or gaining acceptance for a novel doctrine; it is rather that of getting us to take seriously a doctrine that is so familiar that we have forgotten to believe it. 'We, the People . . .'—of course. 'Government by the People . . .'—naturally. 'The sovereign citizens . . .'—certainly. Does this really mean that in addition to the legislative, executive, and judicial branches of our government there is another part of the government, manned by the citizens, charged with the responsibility for making crucial political decisions—a real, concrete tribunal behind the Fourth of July phrase? If it does not mean this it means nothing.

But few things reveal us to ourselves as do our attempts in recent years to interpret and embody in our public life the significance of the Bill of Rights. And what we have revealed is how little a part the conception of The Fourth Branch plays in our daily reckoning. We tend to see the Bill of Rights as designed merely to protect the subject against government, as staking out an area of private rights. We ask, under stress and with regret, whether the necessities of government in an age of peril do not justify some restriction of private freedom. The issue, as we pose it, is between government and the individual, and by 'government' we mean the legislative or the executive branch.

But what is overlooked is that the citizen not only has rights as a private person but has rights or powers as a public official as well. His political powers belong to him as a member of the electoral tribunal, and curbing or infringing those powers radically alters the relation of the Fourth Branch to the other, subordinate, branches of government. For Congress or the Executive to 'supervise' the political activity of the citizen—his speech or his advocacy, his reading or writing—is not simply to assert the priority of public necessity over private expression but to violate the 'separation of powers' at the expense of the independence and dominance of that very tribunal to which we pay such empty rhetorical tribute. There is no greater anomaly in a democracy than the assumption by legislative committees of the role of guardian of the public mind, meddling officiously in the political life of the citizen, wielding its 'un-American' stamp of excommunication. Our toleration of this sort of practice is a measure of our failure to understand the meaning of 'government by the people.' We are quicker to defend our private rights than the integrity of our public function.

There is more to life than politics, even for the political animal. But there is more, also, than the private pursuit of happiness; and nothing is more central to the spirit of democracy than this conviction. The democrat turns his back resolutely on the temptation to divide men into pursuers of happiness and bearers of responsibility. He summons every man to his place in the public forum. To 'life, liberty, and the pursuit of happiness' he adds the 'dignity' which is found in sharing the colleagial life of the rulers of the human city. The threat to that conception of human dignity takes many forms. But none is more deadly than the temptation of the marketplace.

Nature and Politics

Men have seldom thought about the state without attempting to relate it to the broader context of nature within which it is embedded. We begin, it is said, with Zeus or with chaos. If we begin with Zeus the human scene is but a local province in a world which is itself a body politic; if we begin with chaos the human city seems a garden precariously cultivated on the edge of disaster, an ephemeral clearing under siege.

Equally significant for the character of political theory is the persistence and interplay of two attitudes toward the relation of the body politic to nature generally. On one hand there is the tendency to insist on the essential continuity of the natural and the political, to insist that both are to be understood in terms of a single set of categories. On the other hand is the tendency to stress the basic contrast or discontinuity between the realms of nature and politics, to insist on an irreducible dualism which requires a different set of categories for the adequate understanding of each of these disparate realms.

We are early and inescapably confronted with deep contrasts between elements of the social environment with which we are immediately acquainted and the enveloping natural environment, between what is within and what lies beyond the pale. This sense of contrast is well expressed by Hobbes in a famous statement: 'To speak impartially, both sayings are very true; that man to man is a kind of god; and that man to man is an arrant wolf. The first is true when we compare citizens among themselves; and the second, if we compare cities. In the one, there is some analogy of similitude with the deity, to wit, justice and charity, the twin sisters of peace. But in the other, good men must defend themselves by taking to them for a sanctuary the two daughters of war, deceit and violence; that is in plain terms a mere brutal rapacity . . .'

To this sharp sense of the limited range of civility there is soon added the awareness of the varieties of its patterns. The city is not everywhere the same. What is sought here is shunned there, approved here disapproved there.

These two elements, then, the contrast between the city and raw nature, and the contrasts between cities, lie at the core of the distinction between nature and convention, nature and culture, the natural and the polis-like or political.

But this distinction does not hold the field alone. For while we are aware of contrast we are also aware of continuity with nature and natural processes. What is sometimes the enemy also sustains us. It is nourishing and healing. It involves us in its cycles and processes. We are among its animals. And growing out of this there is a rejection of the sense of human isolation and alienation from nature, a contrasting mood of 'natural piety.' In this mood human culture is seen as sustained and supported by nature rather than at odds with it.

But what of the varieties of culture, the differences between cities which make sin a matter of geography in what seems to be a quite accidental or arbitrary way? The cultural 'relativity' which so often supports the distinction between natural and artificial is a fact, but not a necessarily brutal one. Customs differ, to be sure. But we soon find ourselves distinguishing between the common and the purely local, between the universal core and the parochial fringe—a distinction which spills over easily into 'essential' and 'accidental,' itself not far from 'standard' and 'approximation' or 'ideal' and 'imitation.' The upshot of this familiar story is that different songs are seen, in the end, as variations on a single theme, the universal discerned in a variety of garbs.

These two moods, then, the awareness of contrast and the demand for continuity, develop side by side. Neither is ever quite extinguished because both are rooted in basic conditions of human experience. The acceptance, as final, of the contrast between the natural and the political is made difficult not only by the mood of natural piety but by the oddly anthropomorphic character of 'understanding' and 'explaining' and by a related and powerful metaphoric tendency in the use of language.

Much of what we call understanding is simply 'becoming familiar with.' In this process the remote, strange, or unfamiliar gets understood when it is seen to be like, in some or in many respects, what is already near at hand and already familiar. Explanation thus involves, in part at least, the application to the unfamiliar of concepts and categories which have already been developed closer to home. The anthropomorphic character of such explanation is an old story, not only as it is expressed in simple forms of animism but also in more sophisticated explanation which still uses notions of 'forces' and regards 'causing' as 'compelling.' The point is simply that we are more immediately aware of ourselves, our inner lives, and our human, familial relations than anything else, and we draw heavily on this awareness in our attempts at understanding the world around us. What we describe we describe in terms initially appropriate to what we are more immediately acquainted with.

Language is thus inevitably used metaphorically. Proper names become universals as Julius Caesar gives his name to a whole class of Caesars. The horseman finds that mountains have saddles; the potter sees the world as clay, the dramatist as a tragedy, the slave as an absolute monarchy. The tendency to apply the language of the family and of civic life in a metaphoric way to the world at large is quite understandable. In the face of this tendency the nature-body politic distinctions tend to get lost. The river not only overflows its banks, it trespasses on the land. The unseasonable is unruly. Law-abiding water always runs down hill. The sun is kept in its path by justice and her handmaids. Nature becomes a body politic complete with sovereign, and the writ runs everywhere. The stranger is my brother, mankind a fraternal commonwealth enjoying natural rights subject to natural law. Thus, seeing ourselves wherever we look, listening to our own echo, we read our local politics into the world.

Metaphor is a powerful tool. It suggests and illuminates. But it can also mislead us into the idolatry of taking a metaphor literally. Philosophy has always been deeply involved in this source of insight and illusion. In its suggestive moments it rides hard the metaphor which, in an analytic mood, it dissolves and banishes. 'The world is a machine,' we are told, and off we go exploring pushes and pulls; 'but only *like* a machine,' we are reminded when we insist there must be a mechanic.

Awareness of metaphor is only the beginning of wisdom, and to suggest that 'natural law' and 'natural rights' are metaphoric is only to strike a preliminary chord. Some insights seek expression in these terms, which, taken literally, may sketch a fairy tale. What these insights are I now turn to consider.

One preliminary caution. I wish to guard against leaving the impression that the urge to continuity is expressed only in the reading into nature of notions relevant to the human community. It has worked both ways. There have been other conceptions of nature than that of a system pervaded by law or justice. Since the early Greek atomists there has been at hand the conception of nature—not altogether lawless to be sure, but dehumanized, mechanical, materialistic—in which, for example, the category of purpose has little or no place, in which mind or consciousness is a puzzling epiphenomenon caught up in mere appearance and 'illusion,' in which the human condition is one of 'normal madness.' The effect of this general view of nature has itself had, at times, drastic effects on the way we think of life within a body politic. A Newtonian view of nature has tended to generate a Newtonian view of society— as a Darwinian view of nature has spilled over into a Social Darwinism. The rejection of dualism may work both ways: the social categories may get applied to nature; the conception of nature may dominate our understanding of society.

The State of Nature

While 'natural law' and 'natural rights' appear to find the essentially civic notions of 'law' and 'rights' present, in some form, in 'nature,' the concept of 'the state of nature' functions chiefly to mark the contrast between conditions within and conditions outside the bounds of a body politic. Persons (including political entities as 'persons') who are not related as members of a body politic are simply in the state of nature.

The general disrepute of this notion is due, I think, to supposing that it refers to some hypothetical primitive condition, golden or bestial, out of which we emerged in the dim past. But the state of nature is not an anthropological hypothesis. It should be understood as referring to an actually existing condition as when, for example, sovereign states confront each other and, claiming sovereignty, do not acknowledge the overriding authority of a common tribunal with adequate power to enforce its decisions. We know this state of nature well; its style of life we call 'cold war'; and our contemporary discussions of the problems of emerging from it into a condition of peace have not moved beyond, if indeed they have achieved, the clarity of Hobbes.

The threat to the quality of human life posed by the existence of a state of nature has always been recognized. We are sharply aware of the difference in behavior expected, or even possible, within a body politic and in a state of nature—between the 'justice and charity' appropriate to the former and the 'deceit and violence' all too normal in the latter. Thus, the distinction between the state of nature and the body politic serves to remind us of the difference between being related as 'sovereigns' and being related as fellow members of a body politic. It poses the question of the relation between cold war morality and civic morality, or even between the 'moral' and the 'political.'

What, then, is the status of morality or of moral rules in the state of nature? There seem to be several possibilities and I will try to present them by use of a simple example. Let us consider the rule or principle, 'agreements should be honored'—a staple item of civic morality—and a number of sovereign states constantly or sporadically in conflict.

The first situation to consider is one in which some or even all of these states deny that 'agreements should be honored' is a valid moral rule having any claim upon their conduct. In this situation the attempt to solve problems by making agreements would be futile or silly.

The second situation is one in which it is acknowledged on all sides that agreements should be honored but, because of special circumstances, it is also held that one may be morally blameless in acting in violation of this rule. The special circumstances usually involve reasons for distrusting the other party's good faith and the absence of an enforcing mechanism sufficient to overcome or nullify the distrust. This, I think, is the situation Hobbes has in mind when he asserts both that 'covenants are always binding *in foro interno*' and that 'covenants without the sword [of justice] are worth nothing.'

A third situation would be one in which all parties recognized that agreements should be honored and, moreover, could be counted on to do so.

Political theorists who have been concerned to point the way from the state of nature to the body politic, from cold war to peace, by agreement, have not lingered long over the first and last of these possibilities. For the first would make the creation of a body politic by agreement impossible; the last—if such a condition existed—would make it unnecessary.

It is the second case which is the most interesting. It can be characterized as a situation in which moral rules are 'recognized' but are not safe to act on. Or, perhaps, 'We recognize and would act upon them, but we cannot trust the others.' In this case—and it is our case—the problem of emerging from the state of nature is that of creating the conditions in which it is reasonable to make and keep agreements. Acknowledging the moral obligatoriness of 'agreements should be honored' is a necessary but not a sufficient condition.

The task of creative statesmanship in a state of nature is essentially the task of creating a context within which it is possible to behave reasonably and morally. A body politic is such a context, and the sufficient conditions it adds to the state of nature are the common authority and the enforcing power.

My chief concern here with the concept of the state of nature is to make the point that it is not pre-historical speculation but, rather, the statement of a problem which will be contemporary as long as there are sovereign states. Now, more than ever, it holds the threat of mutual destruction as all our efforts at security through power produce only universal vulnerability. For us, as for Hobbes, the hope is that reason prodded by fear will lead us out of the state of nature into a condition of civility.

NATURAL LAW

It is necessary first to disengage the lively core of the natural law question from two familiar but misleading associations. The first involves a confusion between a scientific and a moral conception of natural law; the second involves a confusion of natural law (in the appropriate moral sense) with divine commands. The fate of natural law as a political doctrine should not be made to depend on the existence of an 'objective order of nature' on the one hand or the existence of a command-giving deity on the other.

First, then, the distinction between natural law as a scientific and as a moral conception. This is so obvious that only experience leads to the belief that it is necessary to make a point of it. Bishop Berkeley, for example, distinguished two senses of the phrase 'law of nature': (1) a law of nature as 'any general rule which we observe to obtain in the works of nature' and (2) a law of nature as 'a rule or precept for the direction of the voluntary action of reasonable agents.' This is a clear and simple distinction between a descriptive generalization and a moral rule.

When we speak of science as based on a faith in the order of nature or as concerned with the discovery of the laws of nature we do not mean that it assumes the existence of, or seeks to discover, moral rules, but simply that it looks for regularities which can be expressed in convenient formulas. Such laws as it discovers are descriptions. A law may turn out to be inadequate or perhaps false but it cannot be violated (or obeyed for that matter). A moral law, on the other hand, can indeed be violated or obeyed, but it cannot be regarded as true or false. While I shall not labor this distinction some cautions are justified.

First, the discovery of natural laws of the scientific sort has no bearing at all upon the existence or status of the moral sort of natural law. Faith in a scientific order does not require, demand, or support faith in a moral order. The questions are utterly independent of each other.

Second, we must guard against a tendency to convert a description into a moral rule, a tendency into a principle. A familiar example is the fate of 'self-preservation' which, we sometimes hear, is the 'first law of nature.' Some observers of human behavior have purported to find in men a tendency or drive toward self-preservation—a sort of human analogue of momentum. But even if such a behavioral tendency is observed and expressed in a law—'All human beings tend to preserve themselves'—it by no means follows that it makes sense to regard 'preserve yourself!' as a moral rule or natural law in the moral sense.

If we take the tendency to preserve oneself as overpowering, as something about which we have no choice, then the advice is altogether superfluous. It would be like advising me when I fall to fall at the rate at which bodies fall. If, on the other hand, the advice is not superfluous and 'preserve yourself!' is urged upon us in a situation in which we have a choice, then its force or validity does not follow simply from the existence of a general tendency to behave in this way. 'Do what is usually done' is not necessarily the highest wisdom. (The transformation of psychological hedonism into ethical hedonism is another familiar example of this odd tendency.)

The point is, then, that the scientific and moral aspects of the question of natural law should not be confused. I wish, now, to argue that just as the fate of the natural law doctrine is independent of the fate and career of science, its fate also is independent of the fate of religion, although in some versions this may not be the case.

The obvious connection seems to lie in the relation of moral law to divine command, or moral imperative to moral imperator. Positive law is sometimes defined as the command of the sovereign. Under the influence of this conception of law as command it is supposed, analogically, that the existence of a moral law depends upon the existence of a moral commander, so that the question of the existence of natural law becomes the question of the existence of a god who lays down the law. No god, no moral law; no ruler of nature, no natural law. This is a popular enough view, but it is neither necessary nor inevitable.

Consider our earlier example—'agreements should be honored.' The proper interpretation of such statements has long been a matter of heated controversy. On one widely held view this statement should be interpreted not as a statement, having truth value, but as an imperative—the equivalent of 'honor your agreements!'. Such an interpretation might well evoke a 'who said that?' reaction, and this may sometimes be combined with a disposition to regard such commands as binding only if they emanate from a proper authority. On this interpretation and with this disposition it is easy to see how the existence, and obligatoriness, of natural law depends upon the existence of a divine ruler.

But other interpretations are possible and, depending upon the context, even plausible. For example, 'agreements should be honored' might be interpreted as the equivalent of 'if you honor your agreements you will have a long and happy life.' This is not a command, and its significance as a guide to our action does not necessarily turn on belief in god.

It is interesting to note Hobbes's hospitality at this point. After describing such rules as 'conclusions or theorems concerning what conduces to the conservation and defense of themselves' he adds, 'But if we consider the same theorems, as delivered by the word of God, that by right commandeth all things, then they are properly called laws.' In any case, the possibility of alternative interpretations frees the theory of natural law from any necessary dependence upon religion. The theory therefore deserves further consideration from those who otherwise would get off the train (with me) at this point.

Freed of these all too common associations and confusions engendered by the notion of 'law,' what remains of the concept of natural law? The conception of a 'universally valid moral rule'—where 'universally valid' does *not* mean either 'holding universally,' as a scientific law, or 'promulgated by a universal ruler.'

The doctrine of natural law has often been associated with the notion of a higher law to which appeal is made in times of crisis. The appeal to a higher law rests on the belief that even the highest decision-making tribunal within any political system is limited in its authority by rules or principles which it did not create and which it cannot (as a matter of authority, not power) alter.

We are familiar enough with the notion of a hierarchy of laws—local laws defer to state laws, the laws of a state to federal laws where those are pursuant to, or not in violation of, the still higher laws laid down in the constitution. This conception of a hierarchy of laws is easy to grasp when we see it as a simple reflection of an even more obvious situation—the hierarchical relation of decision- or rule-making tribunals. We are constantly, within our legal and political order, appealing the decisions of an inferior tribunal and its rules or rulings to a higher tribunal and its higher rulings. By a simple analogical extension of this familiar situation it is sometimes asserted that the laws promulgated by even the highest tribunal within any system—usually identified as the sovereign—can themselves be challenged in the name of yet a higher law. The distinctive feature of this situation, however, is that in this case the appeal is to a 'law' which is not the emanation of a tribunal. The authority of this higher law must, if it can claim authority at all, be derived from something other than authoritative promulgation. And we are back again to the question of the possible meaning of 'universally valid moral rule.'

The demand for universality suggests a number of things. First, the validity of the rule must be independent of the character of any particular political context. That is, its validity cannot turn on whether a body politic is democratic, or tolerant, or parliamentary, etc. It cannot be universally valid if its validity depends on the existence of conditions which are present only in some bodies politic.

Second, universally valid in this connection cannot simply mean existing everywhere, in all states, as a promulgated item of positive law, as a custom, or even as a universally held moral belief. Universally valid does not reduce to universally existent. Consensus may be a clue, but it is not all. The Stoics, for example, regarded slavery as a universal custom but nevertheless as contrary to natural law. The appeal to natural law does not have simply the force of 'but everybody thinks . . . !' or 'it isn't done anywhere!'.

And finally, universality suggests a consideration more difficult to explain but, I think, quite essential. A rule would lack the necessary universality if certain odd results would appear if *everyone* acted on it. Consider, for example, a rule like 'one should negotiate only from a position of superior strength.' This seems to make sense for us. But if this rule were acted upon universally there could be no negotiation at all.

I turn now to the question of validity. When universal validity is claimed for a rule we are not, I think, simply claiming that it is true. The difference between 'agreements should be honored' and 'agreements are usually honored' seems clear enough to make the point that the procedure by which the truth of the latter is determined is quite unlike the procedure by which we would try to establish the validity of the former. On this basis, perhaps over-hastily, I put aside a possible identification of 'universally valid' with 'true.'

Nor does 'valid' in this context mean 'valid' in the sense in which a conclusion is said to be validly derived from premises. In this familiar use it refers to the quality of an argument or the adequacy of a proof, to whether something properly 'follows' from something else. This sort of validity, familiar to everyone who has been introduced to the syllogism, is not at stake here.

What is involved in the belief that there are rules of natural law which are universally valid is the view that there are rules which have some overriding claim upon our conduct regardless of the local ground rules to which we are subject. But that claim is not to be established either by authorized promulgation on the one hand or by the simple perception of the truth of a statement in a way which ordinarily establishes a claim upon our belief. The latter, nevertheless, seems closer to the mark, for it is characteristic of the natural law tradition that the emphasis is rather upon discovery than upon decision, upon— to use some traditional but troublesome terms—'reason' rather than upon 'will.' The appeal is thus to some cognitively discernible quality of certain rules, to some discernible appropriateness which evokes a response more like the recognition of truth than like a positive emotive reaction to a directive.

Pursuing this clue I turn now to the notion of 'self-evidence,' to the possibility that natural laws are simply 'self-evident' or, so to speak, self-certifying rules. In its simplest sense a statement is regarded as self-evident when, once it is understood, its truth can be seen without further evidence or argument.

Thus, for example, 'Socrates is mortal' is true, but not self-evident; but 'a bachelor has no wife' is self-evident.

It must be obvious that 'all men are created equal' is not self-evident in this sense. The statement in the Declaration of Independence that 'We hold these truths to be self-evident . . .' should probably be interpreted as meaning something like 'we take these things for granted,' or 'we consider this beyond argument' or 'we start with these assumptions or axioms.' This amounts to a rejection of any need to argue the principles in question. But to be beyond argument in this sense is not the same thing as being self-evident.

The trouble is that what may be beyond argument in one context may not be in another. Jefferson might take it for granted that all men are created equal, but it is not incumbent upon anyone else to do so. This sort of self-evidence is all too local; 'universal truths' have a way of shrinking into merely 'our beliefs.' Walter Lippmann in *The Public Philosophy* illustrates this point: '[The rules of natural law] are the laws of a rational order of human society—in the sense that all men, when they are sincerely and lucidly rational, will regard them as self-evident . . . They are the propositions to which all men concerned, if they are sincerely and lucidly rational, can be expected to converge.' But in a following paragraph a shrinkage occurs: 'They are the principles of right behavior in the good society, governed by the Western tradition of civility.'

Nevertheless, the possibility remains that the selection of 'first principles' may not be altogether parochial or arbitrary and that there is a useful and significant distinction between arbitrariness and appropriateness which may well preserve a meaningful core for the conception of natural law. The search for a meaningful conception of moral 'appropriateness' draws impetus and support from a parallel which can be drawn between the cognitive and the moral enterprise. Within each enterprise there is a strong sense of a distinction between success and failure, between the proper and improper. In the one case we speak of truth and error; in the other of good and evil.

But both pairs of terms can, I believe, be regarded as the peculiar expression, within its own domain, of a common, underlying distinction between the appropriate and the inappropriate. Error is an inappropriateness in belief as evil is an inappropriateness in conduct. Each is a kind of mistake marking a flaw in a discipline.

The point is not that 'true' and 'good' are the same or that the pursuit of knowledge and the pursuit of virtue are the same pursuit. But at the very least they share in common a sense of appropriateness which stands opposed to arbitrariness. Each seeks to develop a discipline which counterbalances the sway of the immediacy of opinion and impulse. Each entertains a contrast between subjective and objective, private and public, and tries to chart a course from the former to the latter. Each has its forms of skepticism, solipsism, relativism, and 'idiocy' against which it seeks the consolation of an intellectual and moral community. Neither is content to write 'whim' upon its doorpost.

The suggestion is that the rejection of arbitrariness in the selection of first principles is based on a conception of moral appropriateness. Just as in the cognitive area our axioms—assumed rather than proved to be true—are not chosen arbitrarily or without reasons, so also our moral or political first principles —the higher law—need to meet some tests of appropriateness and are not simply arbitrarily chosen. These tests involve, in one way or another, an avoidance of 'absurdity.'

While the notion of contradiction seems now to be largely reserved for the relation between statements—i.e. two statements or propositions are contradictory if they are so related that one of the pair must be true and the other false—contradiction can be seen as one of a family of notions with a peculiar common quality of self-defeatingness. We seem to frustrate or defeat ourselves if we assert both a proposition and its contradictory. At the threshold of the world of discourse we encounter the rule 'contradiction not permitted,' and if we reject its authority we find ourselves excommunicated from the world of rational argument. To avoid contradiction, then, is to avoid a kind of self-defeating absurdity.

There are, I think, analogous cases of absurdity, not including contradiction in the strict sense, which bear upon the adequacy of rules which commend themselves to us as possible political first principles or rules of natural law. Consider again our familiar example 'agreements should be honored.' Hobbes, in *Leviathan*, regards this as a part of the law of nature and makes an interesting comment: 'So that injury, or injustice, in the controversies of the world, is somewhat like to that, which in the disputations of scholars is called absurdity. For as it is there called an absurdity, to contradict what one maintained in the beginning; so in the world it is called injustice and injury, voluntarily to undo that, which from the beginning he had voluntarily done.'

Hobbes is here noting an analogy between 'doing and undoing' and 'affirming and denying' and finds, quite legitimately I think, a common quality of absurdity in both cases. And the case for avoiding such self-defeating absurdity seems as strong in one situation as in the other.

While the self-defeat involved may well be an individual's there is also involved the defeat or frustration of an enterprise. The obvious point of the story of the lad who falsely cried 'wolf' is that in the end he was not believed when his danger was real. But there is a broader point implicit in the tale: if everyone gives false alarms an alarm system becomes impossible. An individual who does not tell the truth may, in a society in which truthfulness is general, get away with it. But in a society in which lying is general (if there could be one under such conditions) lying becomes impossible because the system of communication breaks down. It is possible to be a liar only as an exception to the general rule. Thus, while 'tell the truth' as a general rule would work, 'lie when it suits you' as a general rule would be self-defeating or absurd if universally adopted.

The test suggested by this example involves a shift from a

particular case to a general rule. The question is not 'could I (or we), as an exception, act on this rule' but 'could the community adopt this rule without absurdity.' But suppose that, confronted with the demand that one should not act on rules which could not be universally followed, one objects: 'I don't care about the others. I intend to treat myself as an exception to the rule.' It is obvious that the principle 'treat yourself as an exception' is itself absurd. If everyone acted upon it, a system of rules—a community under law—is impossible, and there would be nothing to be an exception to.

A strong case can be made that 'Don't treat yourself as an exception' ('all men are created equal'?) stands at the threshold of moral and political life in the same way that 'don't contradict yourself' stands guard over the realm of discourse and argument. It seems, that is, to be one of those 'natural laws' or first principles, a recognition of which is basic to the enterprise, the rejection of which, in the light of that enterprise, is self-defeating and absurd. It is therefore not arbitrarily chosen but is reasonable or appropriate—a necessary condition or presupposition of political life.

My attempt to find some meaning in the notion of a universally valid, unpromulgated moral rule thus comes to rest with the notion of a rule which is essential to social life in roughly the way that the laws of logic are essential to the life of science or discourse. It rests upon the drawing of a cognitive-moral parallel and the suggestion that 'appropriate' and 'self-defeating' or 'absurd' are primitive notions basic to, and shared by, both domains. The belief in natural law becomes the belief that there are, for the life of the body politic, certain rules whose denial entails the frustration of the enterprise; or, put another way, that political life rests upon certain moral 'presuppositions' or universally valid moral rules—rules whose denial is self-defeating.

I would be content to rest the case for natural law on the status of 'don't treat yourself as an exception!' It is, of course, only a version of the Golden Rule or the Categorical Imperative. It is imperative in form and while it could be stated as 'no one should treat himself as an exception' or 'it is immoral to treat oneself as an exception' many contemporary ethical theorists would hasten to restore, through interpretation, its status as an 'imperative,' and I do not care to argue this question here. (I insist only on the parallel with 'don't contradict yourself' or 'it is irrational to contradict oneself.')

Let it be an imperative, then; but it is not an arbitrary command. It is the necessary imperative of an enterprise and it would, of necessity, be rediscovered if it is ever forgotten. For no community, no body politic, can be created or sustained by its neglect or denial—although here and there, within its protection, a heedless career can run an exceptional course.

To say that there are, or even to adduce, principles or rules which are essential to an enterprise is not to say that everyone will accept that enterprise as one in which he is necessarily involved. If one is prepared to reject the moral or political life, the demonstration that such a life requires 'don't treat yourself as an exception' as its basis does not by itself convert him. Such principles are binding only within the enterprise and only upon participants within it; in the case of moral or political principles, upon members of a moral or political community. Moreover, the discovery of such principles does not remove problems of decision or 'tell you what to do' any more than the principles of logic tell you what to believe or the rules of the road tell you where to go. Natural law should not be regarded as a complete code of conduct, nor rejected simply because it is not. It may be a necessary, but it is not a sufficient guide; and it is quite enough if it can be shown to be relevant to conduct.

But even if this brief analysis has succeeded in making sense of the notion of universally valid rules without identifying such rules either with scientific laws or with divine commands we are still left with the unhappy question—'If *we* act on these rules will *they?* Can we afford to, without the assurance that they will?' The urgency and legitimacy of this question suggests why, notwithstanding natural law, it is necessary to transform a state of nature into a body politic and reinforce the insights of reason with creative acts of will.

Natural Rights

The assertion that there are natural rights seems to be the assertion that there are certain rights which belong to everyone, which are not created or established by the state, and which the state cannot legitimately abolish or ignore. Such rights are sometimes referred to as God-given, but, as in the case of my treatment of natural law, I must put aside this possibility with only a passing comment. This view keeps for natural rights the main features of ordinary rights with only the substitution of God for a determinate promulgating authority. The interesting aspect of the natural rights question, however, is precisely the possibility of giving some meaning to the notion of an unpromulgated, 'unbestowed' right. A metaphoric promulgator does not take us far in this direction.

Let me try to state the problem more clearly. When, living within a political community or legal order, we claim a 'right' we seem to be claiming something that goes along with status in that order and is defined or created by its rules. To say, for example, that I have a right to vote is to say that I satisfy the conditions laid down in the rules which govern voting. More than that, it is implied that I, and others, are so related to those rules as to make them binding upon us—so that what I am entitled to claim others are obliged to respect. And further, it is generally the case that if the exercise of a right is interfered with there is some tribunal with jurisdiction over the matter to which I can appeal for an effective vindication of my claim. All this seems to be involved in the claim to a right within a legal or political order—a system of rules, an organization of individuals acknowledging the authority of those rules, and a tribunal or system of tribunals adjudicating and enforcing claims arising with reference to those rules.

The problem in the case of natural rights is that of making sense of the claim to a 'right' in the absence of some of the distinctive features of the situation in which we ordinarily claim a political right. A right which can be claimed by everyone is not, obviously, a simple fruit of the status of membership in an organization of individuals acknowledging a common authority. A right which is neither created nor alienable by the state is not defined by the system of positive law created and sustained by the state. And a right without a guardian tribunal seems to be that odd entity—a right without a writ or remedy.

The last point offers the least difficulty. In fact, the absence of an adjudicating and enforcing tribunal has seemed to proponents of natural rights, like Locke, to be not an argument against natural rights but rather an argument for the creation of a body politic which would provide the common judge and the common executive power to enforce judgment.

The more difficult questions involve the relation of rights to rules or laws, with the understanding that in the case of natural rights the appeal is *not* to the system of positive law. I shall distinguish and consider two aspects of this situation.

First, to some extent the status of natural rights turns on the status we grant to natural law. If one denies that there are rules of natural law he is hardly likely to accept natural rights as based upon an appeal to that law. But if one accepts natural law there is surely no difficulty about regarding a natural right as a claim to treatment according to its provisions. So that if 'agreements should be honored' is part of the law of nature then parties to an agreement have an equally natural right to performance. In this sense, then, natural law and natural right, whether accepted or rejected, come in a single package.

There is, however, another circumstance from which the conception of natural rights draws some independent strength and meaning. I refer to what might well be called the 'rule-demanding' character of certain situations. We are all familiar with Locke's account of how mixing my labor with a piece of land makes its products 'mine' even in a state of nature. This is the basis of his argument that property is a natural right. 'I made it; it is a product of my labor; it belongs to me' seems on the face of it a plausible enough claim. The theory of surplus value is in good part an expression of indignation at its denial. We may, perhaps, be expressing only a culturally determined attitude, but if we saw people deprived by force of what they had created with their own labor it would evoke a serious 'there ought to be a law' reaction.

It is not supposed that there is a neat, complete, unambiguous system of such compelling claims, but it is the case that the laws we make are, at some points, the reflection or expression of a prior sense of rightness. I say 'at some points' advisedly, for if we consider a whole system of laws we find that much of it prohibits action which would not be regarded as inherently bad. We need traffic rules, but whether we are all to keep to the right or keep to the left is a morally indifferent matter. By contrast, there are areas in which what the law prohibits is regarded, even apart from the law, as bad or immoral.

This sense of thickness at certain points of the legal structure is conveyed also by the distinction between mere legality and moral rightness, and it is this feeling which finds expression in the view that there are natural rights which demand the protection of law. The status of the Bill of Rights is a case in point. As against the view that the entire constitution is 'of a piece'—all parts equally weighty—the 'preferred position' theory holds that some parts of the constitution which embody cherished moral conceptions take precedence, in cases of conflict, over provisions which, however reasonable, lack special moral significance.

In this sense the appeal to natural rights is simply a recognition of the distinction between 'legal' and 'moral' and the insistence that the law accommodate itself to the underlying moral sense of the culture. This is a meaningful demand on any theory of morality except one which deliberately defines justice and morality as 'legality' and denies, on that basis, the possibility that any law might be unjust. Such a theory has its own difficulties.

To say, as is said of a natural right, that it is inalienable is not to say that it cannot be violated but rather that even in the face of persistent violation it retains its claim to recognition. When it is ignored by law, but not in direct conflict with it, it retains whatever claim upon our conduct that moral rules normally have. In the unhappy event of a direct conflict between the demands of law and of moral conviction—as when one is required by law to assist in returning a runaway slave to his owner—the situation takes on a tragic quality. The appeal to Heaven or to conscience on the ground of inalienable rights has seldom been stilled by the Hobbesian reminder that 'the law is the public conscience by which we have agreed to be guided.' But neither are we always willing to face the anarchy of the Protestant conscience run wild. The history of the rebellious appeal to inalienable natural rights is heroic and stormy. And the problems it raises are as unresolved today as when Sophocles probed the mind and heart of Antigone.

Political theory, in its attempts to place the state in its 'natural' context, has been under pressure from two directions, from—if I may speak loosely—science, and from religion. The influence and example of the sciences tempt it toward the description of political life and the search for the natural laws of its movement. But political life is inescapably involved in moral problems, and political theory is thus always entangled with ethics and ethical theory. And here religion raises its standard and invites us to subordinate political theory to theology. Political theory will, because of its ethical component, always resist reduction to 'political science'; but, resisting this, it need not accept the over-eager embrace of theology or religion. Ethical and political theory are no less independent of religion than of science.

Ethical or moral theory has, in the political context, frequently taken the form of discussion of natural law and natural rights. The history of that discussion is long and complicated. I have chosen to ignore that history in this brief treatment not because it is unimportant or unilluminating but because we have been so swamped with history that it is hard to see what the issues are.

The contrast between the natural and the political expressed in the concept of the state of nature reminds us that the body politic is a human artifact making possible, within its bounds, a way of life we call civilization. It reminds us that peace and justice are achievements in the face of natural tendencies and that the conquest of nature is, in its most urgent form, a political problem. The conceptions of natural law and natural right remind us that the political is always in danger of sinking into the 'merely political' and that our political arrangements need to reflect more than whim. They stand, in fact, for the denial of the autonomy of politics and for the subordination of the political to the moral.